NEW THINKING
IN **TEFL**

THE DOLPHIN

General Editor: Tim Caudery

21

NEW THINKING
IN TEFL

Edited by Tim Caudery

AARHUS UNIVERSITY PRESS

Word-processed at the Department of English, Aarhus University
Printed in Denmark by Special-Trykkeriet Viborg a-s
Published with financial support from Aarhus University Research
Foundation

Editorial address:
The Dolphin
Department of English, Aarhus University
DK-8000 Aarhus C

Distribution:
Aarhus University Press
Building 170, Aarhus University
DK-8000 Aarhus C

ISBN 87 7288 371 5
ISSN 0106-4487
The Dolphin no. 21, autumn issue 1991

Subscription price for one year (two issues):
Europe 198 DKK, Overseas US$ 38.00.
Single copy price (not including postage):
Europe 118 DDK, overseas US$ 19.65.
Back issues available - list sent on request.

Contents

Preface

When I was given the opportunity of editing a book on TEFL, I considered looking for some single topic within the field, or a single aspect of a single topic, on which to collect articles. But I soon realised that I would prefer to publish a wide-ranging collection of pieces, reflecting through its diversity the range of areas of study within the field of TEFL. I have not aimed to produce a comprehensive overview of the TEFL field – that would be impossible in a book of this length, or indeed in any single volume – but rather to present a series of insights into varied studies being carried out by people working within the profession. It is my hope that readers will find something of interest in each of these articles, whatever their own particular roles and specialisations within TEFL.

The contributors to this book were asked to suggest topics on any subject of current interest to them, with the only proviso that 'one off' teaching ideas, i.e. teaching suggestions that related to only one lesson or very narrow range of lessons, were to be excluded. The range of studies in this book, then, is considerable, not only in terms of topic, but also in terms of type: there are reports of new empirical research, there are descriptions of types of teaching material and teaching techniques, there are surveys of research literature, there are essays.

Chris Moran's article on lexical inferencing should lead us to use the time-honoured instruction to students to 'work out the meaning of new words from the context' with considerable caution. Judith Munat's first article describes a testing technique for reading comprehension which could be used in many contexts outside university teaching, where it was developed. The article by Brenda Sandilands surveys recent research on teaching writing and is an invaluable guide to the field. Hans Arnt and Althea Ryan discuss the principles behind a suggested approach to teaching writing, and Shirley Larsen's article on teaching and testing writing proficiency at university level describes, among other things, how these principles have been important in the development of teaching materials. Judith Munat's second article takes us into the area of teaching English for Specific Purposes – though in a context perhaps not often considered, the teaching of English for the study of literature. Stephen Keeler introduces the Mini-Saga, a relatively new writing form which can be used in many ways in the language classroom. Anna Trosborg's study of the speech of non-native speakers of English when making requests demonstrates clearly the need to ensure that students have the opportunity in the classroom to learn and practise appropriate language and strategies for interaction. Don Porter and Shen Shu Hung describe a study of the different scores gained in interview tests in relation to different types of language used by the interviewers; it will provide much food for thought for anyone involved in oral examining. David Vale writes about the teaching of young children in an article which will surely be of interest to teachers of students of any age. Glenn Fulcher's article demonstrates through the use of statistics that teachers are able to reliably assess qualities in their students' language that conventional examinations fail to bring out. Robert Wilkinson challenges our assumptions about the language that we teach, noting changes that occur in English when it is used as the European language of business communication. Finally, my own essay discusses some of the ways in which language teachers make use of language teaching theory.

I would like to express my gratitude to everyone who has helped to make this book possible: to the contributors for their generosity in allowing me to publish their work, and for their labours in producing the papers; to Signe Frits, who has laid out the text, patiently coping with numerous complex tables and diagrams and with my editorial shortcomings; to the publisher, Aarhus University Press; to the Aarhus University Research Foundation, who have contributed generously to the financing of this publication; and to my family and my colleagues, who have not complained too strenuously when work on this project has kept me from doing other things. I would also like to mention the Centre for Applied Language Studies at the University of Reading, since it is through that organisation that I know or have been put in touch with many of the contributors.

Tim Caudery

Airports or Whorehouses? Some Problems with Lexical Inferencing

Chris Moran

1. Introduction

The value of lexical guessing or inferencing in teaching reading seems almost to have acquired the status of a dogma. The strategy, which requires readers to make informed guesses about the meaning of unknown words, is widely seen as an essential element in reading comprehension in both first and second languages. Davis (1972) and Spearitt (1972), for example, in their attempt to identify discrete L_1 reading skills, see lexical inferencing from context as one of the few such skills which can be reliably distinguished. Lexical inferencing also features widely in L_1 reading materials. All the five primary-grade reading courses for American native-speaking children analyzed by Rosenshine (1980) include training in understanding words in context, while according to Beck *et al.* (1983:177), in the United States 'Textbooks on teaching reading almost universally advise the development of vocabulary through the use of words in context'.

The situation is similar in second language reading. Authorities on second language reading pedagogy such as Bright and McGregor (1970), Grellet (1981) and Nuttall (1982) all emphasize the vital importance of lexical inferencing. Alderson and Alvarez (1977:3) have such enthusiasm for lexical inferencing that they advise 'encouraging students to throw away dictionaries'. It is scarcely surprising, therefore, that the great majority of reading coursebooks in EFL in both the US (Haynes, 1984) and the UK (Moran, forthcoming) feature training in lexical inferencing. It is the purpose of this article to review the evidence on which this almost universal belief in the value of lexical inferencing is based.

2. The background to research

The popularity of lexical inferencing as a reading strategy has been fostered by a series of related developments in second language research over the last twenty years. First, lexical inferencing has come to be seen as an important cognitive skill in its own right. Sternberg and Powell (1983:882) regard verbal comprehension as an integral component of intelligence and claim that 'individual differences in verbal comprehension can be traced in large part to differences in people's ability to exploit contextual elements that facilitate learning and in their ability to be wary of contextual elements that inhibit learning'. Carton (1971:57) also makes large claims for the importance of lexical inferencing: 'A language pedagogy that utilizes inferencing removes language study from the domain of mere skills to a domain that is more closely akin to the regions of complex intellectual processes'. He links this view to a rejection of the audio-lingual emphasis on 'mimicry and memory', which he argues 'leave little room for doubtfulness and temporary inaccuracies' (p. 56). Honeyfield, too, commends lexical guessing as part of 'an active searching and thinking process' (1977:319).

This view of reading as an active process is also associated with the concept of reading as 'a psycholinguistic guessing game' originated by Goodman (1967). Goodman argued that the fluent reader uses semantic and syntactic information from the context to predict and anticipate meaning and facilitate word identification. Goodman's view determined the direction of much early research into second language reading, as researchers attempted to establish whether L_2 readers also utilized such syntactic and semantic cues (Yorio, 1971; Clarke and Silberstein, 1977; Clarke, 1979; Cziko, 1978; Coady, 1979; Mcleod and Mclaughlin, 1986). Goodman is sometimes cited in support of the proposition that contextual cues facilitate lexical inferencing (see for example Li, 1988). This is despite the fact that his research, which was concerned largely with the word identification strategies of fluent readers in oral reading in L_1, is of uncertain value in studying the lexical inferencing strategies of L_2 readers during silent reading.

Another development which has led to renewed interest in lexical inferencing is the growing body of research into learning styles and strategies. With regard to learning styles, researchers such as Naiman et al. (1978) and Rubin (1975) have claimed that language learning is facilitated by those qualities such as the willingness to take risks and to tolerate uncertainty which are essential to lexical inferencing. Rubin has pointed out that 'the good language learner is a willing and accurate guesser' (1975). A similar claim is made with regard to learning strategies. Rubin (1987) cites Carton's work on lexical inferencing as the starting-point of research into learning strategies, and she suspects that 'inductive and deductive inferencing are the most critical processes in language learning' (1981:122). Such ideas are not restricted to second language research.

Beaugrande (1984:17), in his discussion of lexical inferencing, cites Seymour Papert in support of his argument that

> We should expect errors and accept them as provisional stepping-stones toward better approximations. The reader is always in some danger of confronting unknown items or patterns. The blocking of processing by giving up whenever no certain 'right' answer comes to mind is detrimental to learning of any kind.

Recent developments, however, are perhaps less favourable to the uncritical acceptance of the value of lexical inferencing. Research in L_1 reading, for example, has re-emphasized the importance of the rapid, precise recognition of features, letters and words, and there is general agreement that fluent reading depends more on bottom-up processing of print than on exploiting contextual cues (Stanovich, 1980). Indeed, it appears that it is poor readers rather than good readers who make use of guessing strategies in identifying words in L_1 reading. According to van Dijk and Kintsch (1983:24),

> It has been found over and over again that the best discriminator between good and poor readers is performance on simple letter and word identification tasks. What is really wrong with poor readers is that they recognize isolated words inaccurately and too slowly, and compensate for their lack in decoding skills with context-dependent guessing or hypothesis testing.

These findings, of course, concern word identification in L_1 and cannot be extended to lexical inferencing in L_2. Nevertheless, they suggest that we should perhaps be more cautious when praising the guessing and risk-taking styles and strategies of L_2 readers.

A similar caution is perhaps advisable with regard to some of the more extreme claims made for lexical inferencing. Beaugrande (1984), for example, subjected learners to an experimental training programme aimed at developing 'fuzzy processing', by which he means comprehension based on 'approximations and intuitive guesswork' (p. 18). He trained learners with little knowledge of German to exploit 'the cultural and historical relatedness' of the L_1 (English) and the L_2 (German). Learners were given texts in German and asked to guess the unknown words. One of the sentences read: 'Sie bauten Häuser, Kirchen, Bäckereien, Drogerien, Flugplätze, und Bierhallen'. Beaugrande was certainly tolerant in his acceptance of guesses: 'The student who rendered "Drogerien" as "dog pounds" was in the right semantic field, though applying fuzzy sound/letter correspondences a bit too freely' (p. 22). Nevertheless, even he was disconcerted by the responses to 'Flugplätze',

> which I hoped would be guessed as 'flight places', i.e. 'airports'. However, this association was remote enough that I obtained an extremely wide spread of other guesses: 'flagpoles', 'food plazas', 'fireplaces', 'fluid plants', 'food and plates', hence 'restaurants', and 'floozy places', hence 'whorehouses'.

His enthusiasm for 'fuzzy processing', however, remained undimmed: 'Nonetheless, these guesses indicated an honest effort in comparison to simply giving up on an unknown word and leaving a blank'. Less committed believers in the virtues of 'fuzzy' lexical inferencing might be forgiven for thinking that this is taking tolerance for error too far.

3. Lexical inferencing in first language reading

3.1. Learning word meanings from context

The idea that readers can make effective use of context cues to infer word meanings and acquire vocabulary is, of course, not new. In his classic text (1908:333), Huey stated that when learning to read, the words a young child knows 'help him conjecture what the new words must be, and he enlarges his vocabulary for himself by the use of context, just as he did earlier in learning spoken language'.

The problem is that research which investigates to what extent children learn (rather than guess) the meaning of words from context has by and large failed to find experimental evidence that such learning takes place. The exception is the study by Nagy *et al.* (1985), who found small but significant gains in word knowledge derived from context. Their findings, however, do not conflict with the conclusions of Schatz and Baldwin (1986) that for any given instance, the probability of identifying the meaning of a low-frequency word is very low.

In the absence of clear experimental evidence that L_1 readers acquire vocabulary from contextual guessing, proponents of this view fall back on the argument that the number of words required to read efficiently

> could not be acquired from direct instruction nor from looking them up in a dictionary. There is only one other possible source of knowledge: inference based on context. Thus, logic forces the conclusion that successful readers must learn large numbers of words from context, in most cases on the basis of only a few encounters (Nagy and Anderson, 1984:327).

The problem with this 'default' argument is that it is not clear how large the vocabulary of the average reader actually is. As Anderson and Freebody (1981) point out, it is difficult, if not impossible, to estimate the number of words an individual knows. Estimates of the number of words known by mature readers have ranged from 3,000 to over 200,000 (Goulden *et al.*, 1990). In addition, it has been claimed that good readers can comprehend texts without paying attention to individual words (Smith, 1971) and that 'readers can encounter a substantial number of unfamiliar words in a text with little loss of comprehension' (Nagy and Anderson, 1984:327).

If we cannot establish that readers possess a large vocabulary, or that they need one to understand most texts, it may be that only limited contextual learning of words takes place. However, it is difficult to deny the intuitive plausibility of the view that some readers possess a wide vocabulary and can only have acquired this as a result of learning word meanings from context. As Nagy and Anderson (1984:327) put it, 'the failure to find experimental evidence for contextual learning of word meanings ought to be regarded as a conundrum for experimentalists rather than the basis for educational policy'.

3.2. Lexical inferencing

Direct evidence for the effectiveness of lexical inferencing is provided by Ames (1966) in his attempt to develop a classification scheme of context cues. Ames chose as his subjects twenty native speakers, who were advanced graduate students pursuing doctoral programmes in various fields of education. Twenty texts, on topics of general interest and each over 1,000 words in length, were taken from recent issues of *The Saturday Evening Post* and *The Reader's Digest*. Every fiftieth lexical word was removed and a simulated word with the inflections retained was substituted. Each subject read one of the texts and was then asked to guess the meaning of the simulated word. Ames found that guesses were judged acceptable (i.e. they did not distort the author's intended meaning in the context) in 334 out of 556 contextual situations, 60% of the total.

Some reservations must be noted. In Ames' texts only every fiftieth word was replaced, thus allowing the subjects a large amount of context from which to guess. The simulated words were also inserted at mathematically-defined intervals. Neither of these features are likely to be characteristic of the problems faced in normal reading, and would almost certainly have inflated the number of words guessed. Further, it seems doubtful that the use of simulated words in the study accurately reflects the problems faced by less practised readers in dealing with real unknown words. For example, proficient L_1 readers can use their knowledge of such features of words as the restrictions on the collocational or syntactic patterns into which they enter to guess the meaning of simulated words, especially where the simulated words replace high-frequency lexis. Such knowledge is unlikely to be available for readers when faced with genuinely unknown low-frequency words (Schatz and Baldwin, 1986). This point also applies to research into vocabulary learning based on the responses of native speakers of English to the simulated words belonging to the invented language called 'nadsat' in the novel *A Clockwork Orange* by Anthony Burgess (Saragi *et al.*, 1978).

Both Ames' study and the arguments of Nagy and Anderson referred to above suggest that, given sufficient context, proficient readers can derive the meaning of a significant, though indeterminate, proportion of words in texts of general interest in their L_1. The assumption is then made that this applies to L_2 reading. Seibert (1945:296) makes explicit the often implicitly held belief that the argument for lexical guessing in the mother tongue can be extended to the second language: 'Surely if many words can be acquired from a context in our mother tongue, we can assume that the same mental processes could be used in reading a foreign language'. Similar views are expressed in Nuttall (1982).

However, contrary to the implied view of Nation and Coady (1988) in their recent survey of vocabulary and reading, the applicability of L_1 research to lexical guessing in a second language cannot be taken for granted, as there are a number of important differences between first and second language reading. For example, fluent readers in L_1 typically come across unknown words infrequently in a given text and their ability to access the other words in the text in lexical memory and process syntactic and rhetorical structures efficiently permits them to devote attention to the semantic problems posed by the unknown word. Second language readers, on the other hand, may face multiple linguistic and cultural difficulties when reading texts in a second language and such difficulties may prevent them from allocating cognitive resources to exploiting cues available in the context to derive word meaning.

Another difference is that first language learners meet unknown words repeatedly and in a variety of contexts, thus (presumably) gradually confirming and refining previously tentative guesses. First language readers may be exposed to many millions of words a year (Nagy and Anderson, 1984:328, estimate that 'the figure for the voracious middle grade reader might be 10,000,000 or even as high as 50,000,000'.) The supposition that such extensive reading is a pre-condition for developing lexical inferencing skills is supported by the finding of Jenkins *et al.* (1989) in their study that instruction in deriving word meaning was ineffective with small amounts of practice. It seems unlikely that the limited reading undertaken by most L_2 readers can provide them with similar opportunities for the practice of lexical inferencing skills.

4. Lexical inferencing in second language reading

Given that the results of research into lexical inferencing in first language reading cannot necessarily be extrapolated to second language reading, we would expect that evidence from second language research might provide some support for the favour in which lexical inferencing is held. However, only a few such studies exist.

Seibert's (1945) study is often cited as evidence for the claim that it is possible to guess a large number of words from context in a foreign language (see for example Clarke and Nation, 1980). Seibert's subjects, 48 native speaker college freshmen, read two texts in English from which words and expressions considered guessable from context had been removed, and were asked to fill in the resulting blanks. She found that the maximum number of words guessed was 73% and the average was 60%.

It is doubtful, however, whether this study demonstrates that 'a large proportion' of unknown words can be guessed from context (Clarke and Nation, 1980:211). First, the words to be guessed were not selected at random but were chosen for the reason that they were guessable. If other words had been selected, the number of words guessed would have been lower. Second, the response of L_1 readers to a modified cloze procedure (like their response to simulated words) bears only a partial resemblance to the responses of second language readers to real unfamiliar, low-frequency words (see Haynes, 1984 for similar comments on the utilization of cloze procedures in L_2 reading research).

Liu and Nation (1985) investigated the ability of second language learners to guess unknown words from context. Their subjects, 59 teachers of English as a second language attending a diploma course, were asked to read texts in which low-frequency words were replaced with nonsense words – in the ratio of roughly one in ten words in a short passage and one in twenty-five in a longer text. The total number of correct guesses for the short passage was 23.4% and for the long passage 34.3%.

It is, however, difficult to determine the value of the study, for the following reasons. In the first place, the subjects included 'a few native speakers of English'. The number is unspecified, but could clearly have influenced the results. Secondly, little information is given either as to whether the text was at an appropriate linguistic level for the subjects or as to the background knowledge of the subjects in relation to the text, which was on the subject of economics. Thirdly, the number of words to be guessed was limited to 27 over the two passages. Fourthly, the use of nonsense words, as the authors themselves admit, may have inflated the number of words guessed.

What is clear is that the study demonstrably fails to prove that L_2 readers can guess a high proportion of unfamiliar words from context. It is therefore quite surprising to find this study quoted (along with that of Ames), in the most recent survey of the subject, in support of the thesis that guessing from context is an effective strategy for L_2 readers: 'Liu and Nation (1984), working with advanced second language learners, found that the high proficiency learners guessed between 85 per cent and 100 per cent of the unknown words' (Nation and Coady, 1988:103-4). This is misleading. Liu and Nation identified five of the thirty-four subjects who correctly guessed 50% or more of the non-sense words as high proficiency learners. If any one of these five subjects correctly guessed a word, this was taken as evidence that the word could be guessed. In the short passage, 12 out of 14 words were guessed correctly at least once, thus giving a figure of 85%. Thus, as Liu and Nation clearly point out, it was not *individual* high proficiency learners who could guess 85% of the words from context, but *groups* of such learners. The proportion of correct guesses by this group of subjects was 57%. Liu and Nation unfortunately do not mention whether the high proficiency group contained any of the native speakers. With only five subjects in the high proficiency group, the inclusion of even one skilled native speaker reader could invalidate the findings.

Bensoussan and Laufer (1984) also studied the success with which L_2 learners were able to guess words from context. Their subjects, 60 first year university EFL students studying in different departments, were given a list of 70 words to translate into their L_1 (Hebrew). A week later, they were given a copy of the same list together with a 574-word text entitled 'What is Man?' which contained all the words. They were asked to translate the words again. The researchers then compared the two lists to determine how far the context supplied by the text had helped students to translate the words.

They found that from a total of 70 words, 42% were unguessable from the context; 34% were potentially guessable but were not in fact guessed by the students; and that only 24% of the words were correctly guessed. The proportion of responses in which the subjects made correct guesses, or guesses which did not distort the sense of the context, was even lower – 13%. Bensoussan and Laufer concluded that 'On the whole, lexical guessing was not meaningfully helped by context' (p. 25).

It should be noted, however, that there are some weaknesses in the design of this study. For example, the researchers seem to have chosen a text which many of the students found difficult: 'The weak and average students could not answer comprehension questions on the text without extra-textual vocabulary aid such as a teacher and/or a dictionary' (p. 22). This is a serious defect. It is quite easy to induce students to make 'wild guesses' (one of the researchers' categories) if the text they are reading is too difficult. In addition, requiring students to first translate the words in isolation may not have been an appropriate way of investigating prior knowledge of word meaning. Subjects might have had some knowledge of the word meaning without being able to supply a translation. There are many intermediate stages between firm grasp of the core meaning of a word and absolute ignorance. The design of Bensoussan and Laufer's study, however, does not appear to be powerful enough to capture these complexities.

However, while the precise proportion of words which can be guessed is open to question, the conclusions of Bensoussan and Laufer seem plausible:

lexical guessing is a very difficult task either because of the complexity of the text or because of the limitations of the reader, or both. Some words do not have clues in the text in which they appear; when there are clues for such words foreign language learners will not necessarily look for them; and when readers do look for these clues very often they cannot locate or understand them (p. 27).

More evidence for some of the problems involved in lexical inferencing is to be found in recent research which investigates the strategies second language readers adopt when they attempt to infer the meaning of unfamiliar words. The data in these studies is frequently obtained by asking readers to think aloud or introspect during or immediately after reading a text.

The main finding of this research is that learners seem to be unable to infer word meaning very efficiently, even where clues to the meaning exist. Learners appear to find particular difficulty in exploiting clues which require the students to integrate information across a whole text, rather than those to be found in the immediate context (Haynes, 1984; see also Haastrup, 1985). Instead, they prefer to base their guesses on the form of the word in isolation from the context. This leads to errors. For example, learners are misled by false cognates (Haynes, 1984; Bensoussan and Laufer, 1984). Several Spanish speakers in Haynes' study, for example, misled by the Spanish word *campo*, interpreted *campfire* as meaning *battlefield*. Learners also make mistaken inferences on the basis of morphology (Haynes, 1984; Bensoussan and Laufer, 1984; Parreren and Schouten-van Parreren, 1981). For example, more than half the subjects in Haynes' study guessed that *offspring* meant *end of spring*. More surprisingly, learners tended to access the wrong word in lexical memory because of its graphemic or phonemic similarity to the unknown word (Haynes, 1984; Laufer and Sim, 1985). Thus *tapped* was confused with *top* in Haynes' (1984) study. The result of these false inferences was that learners often misinterpreted the whole text. The general picture to emerge from these studies is that lexical inferencing is an extremely difficult strategy for many learners to operate.

To summarize, it appears that there has been surprisingly little empirical second language research into lexical inferencing and the few studies which exist fail to provide convincing evidence as to the effectiveness of the strategy. The importance accorded to the strategy in pedagogical handbooks and reading coursebooks appears, in fact, to be an act of faith (probably originating in the 'default argument' for L_1 vocabulary acquisition) rather than a rational decision based on firm empirical evidence.

5. Classroom implications

What are the implications of these remarks for teachers and materials writers? First, it appears that lexical inferencing has a more limited role to play in reading than is sometimes claimed. More attention should be paid to an integrated strategy for dealing with unknown words which includes training students to distinguish words which can be ignored, those which can be guessed, and those which are best looked up in a dictionary.

Second, learners seem to find lexical inferencing difficult in both L_2 and L_1 (Jenkins *et al.* 1989). Training should therefore be principled and systematic and go beyond merely exhorting users to use the context to derive word meaning, as frequently happens in reading coursebooks (Alderson and Alvarez, 1977; Moran, forthcoming).

Third, it seems likely that second language learners, like first language learners, need a great deal of practice before they become efficient in the strategy. More emphasis should perhaps be laid on extensive reading, particularly of reading materials with heightened redundancy which might provide learners with enhanced contexts from which to derive word meaning.

Fourth, materials need to be carefully designed to ensure that learners can in fact derive the meaning of words which feature in lexical guessing exercises. Texts need to be selected in which the density of new words is not too high. There is a case for following the American example (Haynes, 1984) and using specially-constructed rather than authentic texts in the classroom, as well as in extensive reading material.

Fifth, in terms of teaching procedures, teachers should perhaps be prepared to pre-teach more lexical items than is fashionable. Perhaps they should also be more prepared to respond to student requests to explain the meaning of a word than they sometimes are. More work on vocabulary building based on texts might also have a beneficial effect on students' reading abilities.

Finally, in the absence of convincing research evidence, we should perhaps be more careful about claiming that the meaning of a large number of words can be guessed, or about advising our students to throw away their dictionaries.

References

Alderson, J.C. and Alvarez G. 1977. *The Development of Strategies for the Assignment of Semantic Information to Unknown Lexemes in Text*. Mexico City: Centro de Ensenanza de Lenguas Extranjeras.

Ames, W.S. 1966. 'The development of a classification scheme of contextual aids', *Reading Research Quarterly* 2, pp. 57-82.

Anderson, R.C. and Freebody, P. 1981. 'Vocabulary knowledge', in Guthrie, W.T. (ed), *Comprehension and Teaching: Research Reviews*. Newark: International Reading Association, pp. 77-117.

Beaugrande de, R. 1984. 'Reading skills for foreign languages: a processing approach', in Pugh, A.K. and Ulijn, J.M. (eds), *Reading for Professional Purposes*. London: Heinemann, pp. 4-26.

Beck, I., McKeown, M. and McCaslin, E. 1983. 'All contexts are not created equal', *Elementary School Journal* 83, pp. 177-181.

Bensoussan, M. and Laufer, B. 1984. 'Lexical guessing in context in EFL reading comprehension', *Journal of Research in Reading* 7, pp. 15-32.

Bright, J.A. and McGregor, G.P. 1970. *Teaching English as a Second Language*. London: Longman.

Carton, A. 1971. 'Inferencing: a process in using and learning language', in Pimsleur P. and Quinn T (eds), *The Psychology of Second Language Learning*. Cambridge: Cambridge University Press, pp. 45-58.

Clarke, D.F. and Nation, I.S.P. 1980. 'Guessing the meanings of words from context: strategy and techniques', *System* 8, pp. 211-220.

Clarke, M. 1979. 'Reading in Spanish and English: evidence from adult ESL learners', *Language Learning* 29, pp. 121-150.

Clarke, M. and Silberstein, S. 1977. 'Toward a realization of psycholinguistic principles in the ESL reading class', *Language Learning* 27, pp. 48-65.

Coady, J. 1979. 'A psycholinguistic model of the ESL reader', in Mackay, R., Barkman, B. and Jordan, R. (eds), *Reading in a Second Language*. Rowley, Mass.: Newbury House, pp. 5-12.

Cziko, G.A. 1978. 'Differences in first- and second-language reading: the use of syntactic, semantic and discourse constraints', *Canadian Modern Language Review* 34, pp. 473-89.

Davis, F.B., 1972. 'Psychometric research on comprehension in reading', *Reading Research Quarterly* 7, pp. 628-678.

Dijk, T. van and Kintsch, W. 1983. *Strategies for Discourse Comprehension*. New York: Academic Press.

Dubin, F. 1989. 'The odd couple: reading and vocabulary', *English Language Teaching Journal* 43, pp. 282-287.

Goodman, K.S. 1967. 'Reading: a psycholinguistic guessing game', *Journal of the Reading Specialist* 6, pp. 126-135.

Goulden, R., Nation, P. and Read, J. 1990. 'How large can a receptive vocabulary be?', *Applied Linguistics*, 11/4, pp. 341-363.

Grellet, F. 1981. *Developing Reading Skills*. Cambridge: Cambridge University Press.

Haastrup, K. 1985. 'Lexical inferencing – a study of procedures in reception', *Scandinavian Papers on Bilingualism* 5, pp. 63-86.

Haynes, M. 1984. 'Patterns and perils of guessing in second language reading', in Handscombe, J. Orem, R.A. and Taylor, B.P (eds), *On TESOL 83: The Question of Control*. Washington: TESOL, pp. 163-176.

Honeyfield, J.G. 1977. 'Word frequency and the importance of context in vocabulary learning', *RELC Journal* 8, pp. 35-42.

Huey, E. 1908. *The Psychology and Pedagogy of Reading*. Cambridge, Mass: MIT Press.

Jenkins, J.R., Matlock, B. and Slocum, T.A. 1989. 'Two approaches to vocabulary instruction: The teaching of individual word meanings and practice in deriving word meaning from context', *Reading Research Quarterly* 24, pp. 215-235.

Kruse, A.F. 1979. 'Vocabulary in context', *English Language Teaching Journal* 33, pp. 207-213.

Laufer, B. and Sim, D.D. 1985. 'Taking the easy way out: non-use and mis-use of cues in EFL reading', *English Teaching Forum* 23, pp. 7-10, 20.

Li, X. 1988. 'Effects of contextual cues on inferring and remembering the meanings of new words', *Applied Linguistics* 9, pp. 402-413.

Liu N. and Nation, I.S.P. 1985. 'Factors affecting guessing vocabulary in context', *RELC Journal* 16, pp. 33-42.

McLeod, B. and McLaughlin, B. 1986. 'Restructuring or automaticity? Reading in a second language', *Language Learning* 36, pp. 109-123.

Moran, C. Forthcoming. 'Lexical inferencing in EFL reading coursebooks: Some implications of research', *System*.

Nagy, W.E. and Anderson, R.C. 1984. 'How many words are there in printed school English?', *Reading Research Quarterly* 19, pp. 304-330.

Nagy, W.E., Herman, P.A. and Anderson, R.C. 1985. 'Learning words from context', *Reading Research Quarterly* 20, pp. 233-253.

Naiman, N., Frolich, M. Stern, H.H., and Tedesco, A. 1978. *The Good Language Learner*. Toronto: Ontario Institute for Studies in Education.

Nation, P. and Coady, J. 1988. 'Vocabulary and reading', in Carter, R, and McCarthy, M., *Vocabulary and Language Teaching*. London: Longman, pp. 97-110.

Nuttall, C. 1982. *Teaching Reading Skills in a Foreign Language*. London: Heinemann Educational.

Parreren, C.F. van and Schouten-van Parreren, M.C. 1981. 'Contextual guessing: A trainable reader strategy', *System* 9, pp. 235-241.

Rosenshine, B.V. 1980. 'Skill hierarchies in reading comprehension', in Spiro, R.J., Bruce, B.C. and Brewer, W.F. (eds), *Theoretical issues in reading comprehension*. Hillsdale, NJ: Erlbaum, pp. 535-554.

Rubin, J. 1975. 'What the good language learner can teach us', *TESOL Quarterly* 9, pp. 41-51.·

Rubin, J. 1981. 'The study of cognitive processes in second language learning', *Applied Linguistics* 2, pp. 117-131.

Rubin, J. 1987. 'Learner strategies: theoretical assumptions, research history and typology', in Wenden, A. and Rubin J., *Learner Strategies in Language Learning*. London: Prentice Hall UK, pp. 15-30.

Saragi, T., Nation, P. and Meister, G. 1978. 'Vocabulary learning and reading', *System* 6, pp. 70-78.

Schatz E.K. and Baldwin, R.S. 1986. 'Context cues are unreliable predictors of word meanings', *Reading Research Quarterly* 21, pp. 439-453.

Seibert, L.C. 1945. 'A study of the practice of guessing word meanings from a context', *Modern Language Journal* 29, pp. 296-323.

Smith, F. 1971. *Understanding Reading*. New York: Holt, Rinehart and Winston.

Spearitt, D. 1972. 'Identification of subskills of reading comprehension by maximum likelihood factor analysis', *Reading Research Quarterly* 8, pp. 92-111.

Stanovich, K.E. 1980. 'Toward an interactive-compensatory model of individual differences in the development of reading fluency', *Reading Research Quarterly* 16, pp. 32-71.

Sternberg, R and Powell J. 1983. 'Comprehending verbal comprehension', *American Psychologist* 38, pp. 878-893.

Yorio, C.A. 1971. 'Some sources of reading problems for foreign language learners', *Language Learning* 21, pp. 107-15.

Oral Assessment of L₂ Reading Comprehension

Judith E. Munat

1. Introduction: The receptive skills

In testing productive language skills – writing and speaking – the examiner has only to elicit the type of behavior being assessed in the form of a 'product', (i.e., a written text or an oral reply). But in evaluating the so-called receptive skills, those of listening and reading, the problems are greater, since neither of these skills involves an observable result or product. Sensory perception (hearing or sight) of visual or auditory input is the point of departure following which decoding operations[1] and higher order cognitive processes are activated in order that the listener or reader may assign semantic meaning to the linguistic code. Therefore, decoding and comprehension of the message, whether this message is transmitted in phonemes or graphemes, is an unobservable process which goes on in the reader's or listener's mind and as such is not easily measurable.

Although the processing of spoken and written text is, to some extent, similar, listening comprehension is facilitated by the prosodic and paralinguistic features typical of speech as well as by its socially interactive nature and the shared message context between speaker and hearer, whereas reading is a de-contextualized, one-way communication which requires the *a priori* learning of a conventional coding system (quite another skill from the acquisition of the natural coding system of speech which is easily mastered by any child) (Perfetti, 1985). But on the other hand, reading is facilitated by the fact that the reader, unlike the listener, can control the rate of textual input (Just & Carpenter, 1980) and has the possibility of reinspecting the text, thereby reducing demands on memory (Perfetti, 1985). This visual effort (in terms of eye fixations) involved in stopping or going back over text, as we will see, is one of the factors at the base of empirical research into the reading process.

2. Process vs. product of reading

In summary, then, the central processes of reading, according to Perfetti (1985:5), are essentially 'mental operations on linguistic structures that begin with visual input', thereby involving visual, linguistic and mental processes. Psycholinguistic research has attempted to examine these covert processes through the study of such externally verifiable behavior as eye fixations (Just and Carpenter, 1980) or miscue analysis (Goodman, 1969) which, however, give only limited information about what the reader does as he reads. Such studies ultimately tell us little about the mental processes and absolutely nothing about the product of reading, i.e. *what* the reader has effectively understood. We as testers, instead, are primarily, if not exclusively, interested in this product.

How, then, are we to test an invisible product? On the basis of what behavioral manifestations are we to evaluate such an elusive and abstract concept as comprehension? And, further, have we clearly defined our testing objectives? Are we aiming to assess the reader's comprehension of one specific text or are we instead attempting to evaluate his/her ability to comprehend texts in general?

3. Assessment of comprehension

At the present state of the art of testing, the only means by which we can evaluate comprehension is by eliciting a behavioral response from the reader, usually spoken or written.[2] Our reader/test subject must externalize his comprehension in some observable behavioral 'product' in order for us to judge whether the reading process has been successful.

Traditionally, such behavioral response has involved responding to written comprehension questions on a text. In this case the reader must understand not only the text, but the questions as well. He must also, quite possibly, be able to produce a written product in the form of replies to the questions. Are we assessing his ability to comprehend a text, or his ability to communicate in writing? Even in those cases where the test questions require merely a true/false reply or an X strategically placed in front of the correct alternative, can we be certain that a correct answer reflects comprehension of the text and is not simply a good guess, or that an incorrect answer is due to misinterpretation of the text rather than of the question? And, how much of the testee's performance is attributable to more or less successful test-taking skills, such as working well under pressure, efficient allotment of time, etc.?

The foregoing are only some of the primary objections to traditional reading comprehension multiple choice or stem completion tests. And we have not even touched upon the more controversial theoretical question at the basis of test construction: is the reading skill composed of a series of subskills that can be isolated and individually tested (e.g., vocabulary knowledge, prediction, inferencing, etc.) or is it, instead, a unitary skill that cannot be usefully broken down into such subcomponents?[3] To date the research has not provided indisputable evidence for either of these hypotheses and so we can only join one or the other schools of thought and proceed to seek evidence for our position. But all this brings us no nearer to resolving the problems inherent to the testing of reading comprehension.

4. Oral comprehension assessment technique

As a viable and valid alternative to traditional reading comprehension tests, the use of an oral interview conducted in L_1 on a text read in L_2 was studied in an experiment carried out at the University of Pisa. The experimental design and results reported below give evidence that such an oral testing instrument has decided advantages over a written multiple choice reading comprehension test: that of isolating only one L_2 skill – that of reading – and of permitting the examiner to probe global text comprehension without reducing the comprehension skill to a series of mini-strategies or test-taking skills. No answers can be attributed to guessing or to misinterpretation of the questions, since both examiner and reader have the possibility of clarifying anything which is unclear. The communicative validity of such a procedure is also evident in the authentic two-way communication that goes on between examiner and testee. In addition, the examiner's assessment, although based on subjective evaluation, proves, in the final analysis, to carry much the same objective reliability as the numerical scores of a traditional comprehension test if a band scale with descriptive parameters of the examinee's performance is adopted.

5. Report of experimental study

5.1. Subjects

Twenty-five students at the University of Pisa were used as subjects for the following experiment. They had all studied English at school for a minimum of five years prior to university, and were all degree candidates in the Faculty of Letters, enrolled in an English reading course with the goal of acquiring the necessary skills to be able to cope with reading English texts in their various fields of study.

5.2. Experimental design

A standard reading comprehension test (the ELBA) was administered to the group of students and thirty minutes were allowed for completion. The test consisted of four brief texts (75 to 150 words each) representing different text-types (expository prose and instructions) and different topics, none of which were particularly close to the students' fields of study or general interests. There were a total of 20 questions with multiple choice stem-completion items primarily aimed at testing literal comprehension (i.e., based on knowledge of vocabulary, syntax, cohesion and the ability to identify main ideas). The scores were tabulated and the students ranked according to their performance.

The same students were the subjects for the oral interview conducted in a series of individual appointments set up on four separate days in the week following the administration of the written test. The procedure followed was the same for each student: an article from the *Guardian Weekly* was presented[4] and the student was allowed five minutes or more, if required, to read the text, after which the opening questions concerned the general content and text-type. The following questions depended on the student's earlier answers, and thus the direction of the exam was flexible.[5] The chart in Figure 1 summarizes the various possible question-types and classifies them according to function, but the number and type of questions asked in any one interview depended exclusively upon the text being discussed and the student's level of comprehension. A greater number of questions were asked on those parts of the text which appeared to cause the greatest difficulty, in order to establish the nature of the incomprehension, whether code-related or due to conceptual difficulties. Help was given with difficult vocabulary when requested with no negative effect on the final assessment (unless the unfamiliar lexical items were part of a core vocabulary).

The students' performances were ranked according to the band-scale assessment (see Figure 2), and empirical (concurrent) validity was determined by applying the Spearman rank correlation coefficient to the two sets of rankings obtained.

5.3 Discussion of validity

The resulting correlation was .76, which would appear to confirm that the oral assessment was, in fact, measuring reading comprehension (assuming, of course, that the ELBA is a true measure of reading comprehension.)

In addition, theoretical content and face validities were determined, the first on the basis of a practical analysis of test content and the second on the testees' affective reactions.

1. Vocabulary & Idioms	2. Literal Comprehension	3. Reference/Anaphora
e.g. What does ... mean? Can you make a guess based on context?	e.g. Wh- questions How/why Give an example of ...	e.g. What does 'it' refer to? What does 'this' refer to?
4. Paraphrase	5. Analysis	6. Interpretation
e.g. Where in the text does it say that ... ?	e.g. Is there an explanation? a solution? a conclusion? What is it?	e.g. What does the headline mean? (asked before and after reading text).
7. Inference	8. Discrimination	9. Synthesis
e.g. Is the writer for or against? What is his attitude? Whose opinion is this?	e.g. What are the main points? the supporting ideas?	e.g. What is the controlling idea? Summary of text.
10. Text Function	11. Rhetorical Structure	12. Tone/Style
e.g. What is the purpose of the text? Why did the author write this? To whom is it addressed?	e.g. How is the article structured?	e.g. Identify the tone. What textual clues are there?
13. Critical Evaluation	14. Personal Knowledge	15. Personal Opinion
e.g. Is this text inform-ative? Interesting? Why/ Why not? Compare with another text.	e.g. What is the situation in Italy? How does Italian democracy work? What is the curriculum here?	e.g. Do you agree? What do you think about this? Would you like to do this?

Figure 1. Oral exam question types

Content validity was based on a comparative analysis of the question types in the two tests. Those in the oral assessment procedure appeared to give greater coverage of a wider variety of the hypothetical subcomponents of the reading skill (comprising decoding skills at word and sentence level, guessing strategies, inferencing, synthesis and discrimination, activation of content and cultural schemata, etc.) than did the ELBA. The questions on the ELBA, in fact, primarily tested literal comprehension, and 14 out of 20 were code-related (syntactic relations, grammatical transformation, synonym substitution, recognition of lexical cohesion, etc.), not requiring the activation of higher-order reasoning skills or extra-textual knowledge.

Face validity of the ELBA, determined on the basis of student feedback, was largely negative. The students felt that the distractors among the stem-completion alternatives created interference between them and the text, and many of the alternatives were considered to be ambiguous, or even confusing with respect to what had been understood from the text. Also, the text-types were criticized as being 'too technical' and the vocabulary 'too difficult'.

Our subjects, on the whole, reacted more positively to the oral interview, but it must be stated that oral exams are standard in Italian universities so the students were more familiar with the oral procedure. They stated that they felt more 'comfortable' being able to negotiate their replies with the examiner and appreciated being allowed to ask for help with difficult vocabulary.

5.4 Discussion of communicative criteria

The final argument in favor of the oral interview technique was that of communicative authenticity. Foremost among communicative testing criteria is the consideration of authentic tasks and texts. The texts used in the oral exam were authentic newspaper articles (and not texts written for the purpose of the exam), selected because they were believed to be of interest to the students with whom we were dealing; such interest does, in itself, contribute to 'authenticity' of purpose. That is to say, a text which arouses interest approximates a more authentic reading purpose (i.e., reading for interest as opposed to reading exclusively for the necessity of answering exam questions).

In reference to our university context, the task of responding to oral questions is far more 'authentic' than digging through a list of multiple-choice distractors to select the one presumably correct alternative.[6]

The two-way communication which occurs between testee and examiner gives further communicative authenticity to our oral comprehension exam procedure.

6. Use of L_1

The use of L_1 as the 'examination language' in our oral assessment procedure obviously presumes that the testees belong to a monolingual group and that the L_2 teacher has an adequate command of their native tongue, but when these conditions can be met, the use of L_1 offers many advantages.

In Nuttall's words (1982:130), 'It is possible to understand FL texts without being able to express yourself adequately in the FL ... the student may be able to understand both text and questions, but unable to express the answer he would like to give'. Therefore, students can explore text more accurately if they are permitted to use their native tongue in responding, especially when their language learning goals are purely receptive (as in the case of our subjects). Harrison and Dolan (1979) reinforce this claim in stating that, when the examiner is not interested in language production as such but wishes to focus on the content of the passage, there is no necessity for the test to be conducted in L_2; both questions and answers can be in L_1. Further, the use of L_1 serves to reduce anxiety on the part of the test-taker (Shohamy, 1984).

7. Reliability of Bandscale Assessment

Bandscale assessment serves to render the subjective assessment technique more reliable, according to Carroll and Hall,[7] and thus we devised a bandscale describing performance in terms of the examinee's linguistic competence and global comprehension, as well as his ability to employ reasoning skills (see Figure 2). Our intention was to provide a profile of reading comprehension skills which considered both negative and positive criteria at each level and were neither too detailed to be manageable by the assessor nor too simple to give an adequate amount of information upon which to make a decision (see Carroll and Hall, 1985:78), a profile which has the additional advantage of allowing the student to know what his strengths and weaknesses are (whereas a purely numerical cumulative score does not provide such descriptive information).

The eight levels in our bandscale proved to be manageable; more would certainly have been cumbersome. Within the higher levels a 3-point margin of flexibility was allowed (necessitated by the numerical grading system used at the University of Pisa), while at the lower levels a 4-5 point margin was allowed (where a finer discrimination was not deemed necessary). The examiner first selected what was felt to be an appropriate band and then refined his evaluation during successive questioning in order to assign a more precise numerical grade within the band.

| | **BAND SCALE** |
	ORAL ASSESSMENT OF READING COMPREHENSION
28 - 30	Correct information in reply to all (or nearly all) questions; no misinterpretations of content and little or no difficulty with vocabulary.
25 - 27	Generally understood content, but made one or two incorrect interpretations of text; requested some help with difficult vocabulary
22 - 24	Difficulty in identifying main ideas or opinions expressed in text; several incorrect or partially correct replies; obvious difficulties with vocabulary and sentence structure.
18 - 21	Barely sufficient level of understanding; serious gaps in comprehension of details but understood general gist of article.
14 - 17	Serious misinterpretations and difficulties with syntax and vocabulary such as to have missed main points and essential information.
10 - 13	Struggled to pick out isolated facts or vocabulary but unable to piece together general discourse.
5 - 9	Got only occasional vocabulary items; identified basic subject/verb/object structure but no ability to link information.
0 - 4	Generally non-existing English language reading skills. Why bother to take the exam?

Figure 2. Descriptive parameters for oral assessment of reading comprehension.

In the above-reported experiment the experimenter was both examiner and assessor, though it would be useful to employ a two-person team, one doing the questioning while the other applied the assessment criteria, to allow a more accurate assessment and reduce exam fatigue. Finally, if time allowed, a training session for the various examiners in the application of the bandscale would be advisable in order to guarantee greater inter-marker reliability.

8. Practical advantages and disadvantages

As a closing consideration, in addition to the foregoing discussion of the validity and reliability of the oral interview technique, let me make a brief mention of some of the more practical advantages. First, considered in its pedagogic function, as a test of a reading skills the above-described approach to reading comprehension assessment allows the student to spend more time actually reading the text and less time and effort grappling with comprehension questions. (As a case in point, the texts used in our oral interview were longer than those of the ELBA where more time is, instead, spent on reading the questions.)

From the point of view of the examiner, no results can be attributed to cheating! (not a minor consideration in view of the culturally acceptable 'solidarity' among our students). And, from the point of view of the test constructor, the oral interview is more economic in terms of time saved in writing and trialling written test items. Also, there are no problems with replicability because each test is unique, following, as it does, the stream of the student's replies rather than imposing a structure of fixed test items.

The one major disadvantage, in addition to the aforementioned problem of an adequate command of the student's native tongue, is the time factor. Calculating ten to fifteen minutes per student for the oral interview, it is clearly more advantageous in terms of time to administer a written test to the entire group, but if time efficiency is sacrificed to the numerous other advantages in terms of validity and communicativity of the oral assessment technique, we feel that it is time well lost.

Notes

1. Decoding is used here in Goodman's sense of the word, to indicate how graphemes or phonemes are translated into a meaning code. This can be either direct, graphemes to meaning, or mediated, graphemes to phonemes to meaning.

2. Although in theory it would be possible at a rudimentary textual level to elicit other types of behaviour, as for example in the case of a text with instructions to be executed: 'Go sit on the floor under the table'; the reader's subsequent behaviour would indicate whether the message had been correctly interpreted.

3. See Lunzer *et al.* (1979), Wray (1980), and Farr *et al.* (1986) for a discussion and review of the research in reading subskills.

4. Four articles were alternated in the experiment to recreate an authentic exam situation in which different students are given different texts in order to avoid the effect of student 'informers' who pass on information to others waiting to take the exam. The topics of the texts chosen were intended to be akin to the students' fields of interest or general knowledge on the assumption that familiar topic would generate higher interest and this, in turn, would facilitate the application of effective reading strategies (see Olshavsky, 1977).

5. Nuttall (1982), in fact, states that exactly what questions will be asked cannot be planned in advance since these will depend on responses given to earlier questions.

6. In fact, Weir (1988:47) states that answering MC questions is an unreal task because 'normally ... an understanding of what has been read or heard can be communicated through speech or writing'.

7. Carroll and Hall (1985) claim that subjective assessment can be put into the domain of reliable measurement and invoke the use of a band-scale which specifies levels, abilities and descriptions.

References

Carroll, B.J. and Hall, P.J. 1985. *Make Your Own Language Tests*. Oxford: Pergamon.

Farr, R., Carey, R. and Tone, B. 1986. 'Recent theory and research into the reading process: implications for reading assessment', in Orasanu, J. (ed.), *Reading Comprehension From Research to Practice*. Hillsdale, N.J.: Erlbaum.

Goodman, K.S. 1969. 'Analysis of oral reading miscues: Applied psycholinguistics', *Reading Research Quarterly* 5, pp. 9-30.

Harrison, C, and Dolan, T. 1979. 'Reading Comprehension – a psychological viewpoint', in Mackay, R., Barkman, B., and Jordan R.R. (eds.), *Reading in a Second Language*. Rowley, Mass.: Newbury House.

Just, M.A. and Carpenter, P.A. 1980. 'A theory of reading: from eye fixations to comprehension', *Psychological Review* 87/4.

Lunzer, E., Waite, M. and Dolan, T. 1979. 'Comprehension and comprehension tests', in Lunzer, E. and Gardner, K. (eds.), *The Effective Use of Reading*. London: Heinemann Educational Books.

Nuttall, C. 1982. *Teaching Reading Skills in a Foreign Language*. London: Heinemann.

Olshavsky, J.E. 1977. 'Reading as problem solving: an investigation of strategies', *Reading Research Quarterly* XII/4.

Perfetti, C.A. 1985. *Reading Ability*. New York: Oxford University Press.

Shohamy, E. 1984. 'Does the testing method make a difference? The case of reading comprehension', *Language Testing* 1/2.

Weir, C.J. 1988. *Communicative Language Testing*. University of Exeter.

Wray, D. 1980. *Extending Reading Skills*. University of Lancaster.

Approaches to Teaching Writing

Brenda Sandilands

1. Introduction

The enormous amount of research on developing writing skills and the consequent plethora of approaches and materials has provided a complex and frequently contradictory body of literature on the subject. As a result, those involved in any aspect of designing a writing syllabus face a daunting task. It is essential to examine carefully the changes in theory and practice that have taken place, in order to make informed decisions. A close study of the major issues provides course designers with a variety of choices and aids them in selecting those which seem most appropriate for specific situations. The following discussion focuses on developments in the field during the past two decades and devotes particular attention to product-based and process-based approaches to teaching writing skills.

2. The product-based approach

The product-based approach to teaching writing skills goes back a long way, in both the native-speaker and the second/foreign language classroom. Over the centuries, students have learned to write by imitating the style of the renowned authors of their day. Watson (1982:5), referring to the late 18th century, observes that

> people felt that they knew who the best writers were in English and that there was no surer guide to good writing than careful study of and imitation of their products. Thus evolved a tradition which, with a certain increase in sophistication and refinement of the notion of imitation, continues yet in many composition tasks intended for American college students and is particularly strong in second and foreign language teaching.

Thus models have been used as samples of good writing, a target for students to set their sights on. There are other reasons for their widespread use: they introduce a variety of lexical items and a great deal of information about the structures and conventions of the language (Watson, op cit); they allow the student to become familiar with discourse structures (Hillocks, 1987); and they provide insight into foreign standards of rhetoric (Kaplan, 1967). Research carried out by others, notably Sapir and Whorf, makes it clear that models, in particular authentic texts, help the student to perceive and become familiar with aspects of the foreign culture.

How have models been used in the classroom? Traditionally, product-based lessons are organized in much the same way: each lesson begins with a model of the type of text the student is expected to produce at a later stage; there follow a series of exercises, questions and analyses of certain characteristics of the model; and afterwards the student works on producing a similar text. The topic may be different, but the resulting piece of writing should closely resemble the model analysed in class. At the advanced level, the model may be an authentic text (see, for example, Arnold and Harmer, 1978; O'Driscoll, 1984), whereas specially written or simplified texts are usually employed at elementary levels (see Hedge, 1983).

3. A reassessment of models

Clearly, models have provided useful input over the years. However, it has increasingly been questioned whether it is actually possible for students to transfer the characteristics of well-written models to their own work (Corder, 1967; Krashen, 1978; Watson, 1982). In the past, teachers presumably felt certain that the analysis of carefully-chosen pieces of writing provided their students with everything they required in order to become good writers. During the past twenty years or so, however, this certainty has been called into question, as the ever-growing body of research results suggest that the problem is actually much more complex and that more than mere analysis and imitation is required. The focus on imitating models, that is, products written by others, meant that teachers did not look into what students actually did while they were composing. As it became more evident that it was necessary to discover what students did, in order to help them, researchers turned their attention to the behaviours and strategies employed by writers. The resulting research projects, which include individual case studies (see Lay, 1982; Raimes, 1985; Zamel, 1982, 1983), interviews (Emig, 1971; Perl, 1979) and protocol analyses (Arndt, 1987; Flower and Hayes, 1980, 1981; Perl, 1979) have provided important data which has revealed the complexity of the writing process, thereby challenging many of the long-standing beliefs about the nature of writing. The important and influential work of Flower and Hayes has resulted in the creation of a model of the conscious process involved in writing (1981:370), and provided scope for further debate and research.

4. The process-based approach

As the aim of process-oriented research has been 'to explore the underlying processes of composing, the multiplicity of constraints that writers must juggle and orchestrate to produce a text' (Zamel, 1987:698), it is clear that the pedagogical implications are far-reaching. At this point, it is worth taking a closer look at how the process-based approach to teaching writing operates in the classroom.

The teacher who adopts a process-based approach focuses on purpose and content rather than the often mechanical production of compositions. Because it has become important to see writing as a way of communicating with a real audience, teachers are less inclined to use writing as an exercise in language revision. Students, in turn, begin to write for a reader or readers, rather than a teacher who simply corrects errors and assigns a grade. Many researchers (see, for example, Byrne, 1979; Widdowson, 1983), have stressed the importance of the writer-reader relationship. Students are encouraged to read, and comment on, each other's work since 'it is by responding as readers that students will develop an awareness of the fact that a writer is producing something to be read by someone else' (White, 1987:vii).

The concept of the exploratory aspect of writing is crucial: students learn, discover meaning, and solve problems through writing. They also learn procedures for generating ideas and creating appropriate text structures (see Hughey et al., 1983 for a discussion of idea-generating heuristics).

Students also learn to criticise their work and that of their peers (Jacobs, 1987), while developing a concept of writing as 'work in progress' (Zamel, 1987:710) which requires revision and editing. There is thus a move away from the belief that only one draft is required:

> ... traditional instruction ... resulted in student writers who believe that only one draft is necessary and that Whiteout is the writer's best friend, permitting the immediate elimination of the perceived errors. The resulting writing may be cosmetically more appealing, but it is usually superficial and poorly organised and developed.
>
> Hillocks, 1987:80

Students are encouraged to develop a positive approach to revision and to be prepared to adapt their initial writing plan as they discover what they want to say and how they can best express it. Thus, through the use of self- and peer-editing, teacher guidance, and the writing of multiple drafts, students begin to see ongoing revision as an integral part of the writing process.

5. Criticism of the process-based approach

It was perhaps inevitable that the process-based approach, after occupying a central role during the 1980s in debates on teaching compositions, would eventually come under attack. As often happens, the approach has been perceived and interpreted in different ways by various researchers, and has thus been criticised on a umber of grounds. Horowitz, objecting to the 'fashionable' acceptance of the process approach as 'a complete theory of writing' (1986:141), focuses on four main aspects:

> ... its emphasis on multiple drafts may leave students unprepared for essay examinations ... overuse of peer evaluation may leave students with an unrealistic view of their abilities ... trying to make over bad writers in the image of good ones may be of questionable efficacy ... the inductive orientation of the process approach is suited only to some writers and some academic tasks.
>
> (ibid: 446)

Other researchers, however, would reject the above criticism on the grounds that process activities help the student become a more proficient writer who will eventually find it easier to cope with a variety of writing tasks, including examinations. Byrne (1979:112) observes that 'what is important is that students should appreciate the importance, for example, of making notes and drafting. The fact that they cannot always do this when asked to write against the clock in an examination does not invalidate the procedures'. Horowitz has also criticised the process concept of form (as described by Taylor, 1971 and Zamel, 1983), claiming that

> [t]he erroneous assumption here is that writers work in a cultural vacuum, that each writer begins not only with a literal but also a cultural *tabula rasa*. In fact, the form in which a writer expresses meaning owes just as much to the constraints of the writing situation – the genre and the specific demands of the task at hand – as it does to the writer's mental processes.
>
> (Horowitz, 1986:447)

One obvious implication is that researchers and teachers should take into account both the writer's mental processes and the particular requirements of each writing situation. Another is the fact that, as the process approach has been largely concerned with the affective, cognitive and psycholinguistic aspects of writing, it may have partially lost contact with the more down-to-earth requirements of the classroom. In short, teachers must adopt an approach which enables students to cope with the writing assignments they will be expected to produce in the future. Hamp-Lyons (1988) discusses the need for a consideration of product (writing task) before process; this does not, however, mean neglecting the process of writing: '... the student's writing process will therefore be constrained by the "product before", and a task of EAP writing teachers is to reconcile such product restraints with helping students learn to write academically using a process approach' (ibid: 35).

Part of the problem may be due to misunderstanding. For example, Horowitz (1986) challenges statements made by Taylor (1981:8): 'organisation grows out of meaning and ideas' and Zamel (1983:181): 'decisions about form and organization only make sense with reference to the particular ideas being expressed' in order to make the point that we should not ignore the conventions of style and organization or the fact that students must be taught to cope with certain types of writing tasks. However, it is not clear whether the researchers quoted are in fact as removed from reality as is implied; Zamel (1987:708), for example, has referred to 'the misunderstandings about process-oriented instruction' and discussed ways in which 'product goals can be accommodated in nontraditional, student-centred environments'. Moreover, common sense tells us that the extremely valuable insights provided by process research can indeed be useful when dealing with the practical requirements of specific writing tasks. More recent research as well as the application of process theories in some recent writing coursebooks (see Hamp-Lyons and Heasley, 1987; White, 1987) provide evidence of the link between process theories and product goals.

However, in spite of academic enthusiasm for process theories, it has been observed that few of these coursebooks are actually being used and few teachers are changing their approach to teaching writing (Hairston, 1982; Zamel, 1987). There are a number of possible explanations for this phenomenon, ranging from the fact that, while some teachers find it easy to adapt to new materials and approaches, many others are reluctant to do so, to the parallel problem that students, as well, vary in their reactions to different methodologies; some are keen to experiment, whereas others prefer traditional approaches. It is also worth taking into account the fact that many teachers are locked into syllabus and coursebook choices which cannot easily be changed from one year to another, due to financial and/or administrative restrictions. Another prime consideration is time. Many teachers and students feel that, given the limited amount of time at their disposal, it is less time-consuming to use a model-based approach. They may find the process-based approach novel and interesting, but decide that it is far too time-consuming. Of course, if they could be convinced that the extra time spent on such activities as brainstorming, editing and re-writing resulted in better products, there would be more support for the process approach. Further research and wider dissemination of the results may eventually lead to a more widespread acceptance of the value of process theories.

A further explanation is lack of information and/or lack of interest in new developments. Hairston (1982) observed a small group of teachers keep up to date with recent trends:

> ... some of my readers may want to protest that I am belabouring a dead issue – that the admonition to 'teach process, not product' is now conventional wisdom. I disagree.

Although those in the vanguard of the profession have by and large adopted the process model for teaching composition and are now attentively watching the research on the composing process in order to extract some pedagogical principles from it, the overwhelming majority of college writing teachers in the United States ... teach it by the conventional paradigm, just as they did when they were untrained teaching assistants ten or twenty or thirty years ago.

(Hairston, 1982:78)

She attributes this great divide to the fact that a minority of teachers do research, read professional journals and attend professional meetings. She also points out that although many composition teachers originally trained to teach literature or literary criticism, they end up teaching writing out of necessity, rather than interest.

6. The effective writing syllabus

What, then, do our students really need in order to become good writers? And what elements should be included in an effective writing syllabus? Research findings suggest that a lot of writing practice is, in itself, insufficient, as it only seems to lead to improvement in grammatical accuracy (Brière, 1966). Zamel (1976) and Krashen (1984) report similar findings, observing that an increase in writing practice does not help improve composition writing.

On the positive side, there is some evidence to support the view that it is useful to teach students the basics of rhetorical organisation (Shaugnessy, 1977). Sommers (1981), however, in a study of skilled and unskilled writers, concludes that the unskilled writers felt inhibited by the imposition of rhetorical guidelines. Clearly it would seem best to use such guidelines during the final editing stage, rather than at the beginning, so as not to inhibit students during the pre-writing and writing phases.

Hillocks' (1987) important research on teaching writing has significant implications for the FL writing classroom. His comparison of six instructional focuses indicates that the inquiry focus (a method which involves the use of information and strategies for including it in written texts) was responsible for the greatest improvement in the quality of students' writing.

The next most effective focus was sentence combining, a procedure that involves joining two or more sentences. The usefulness of this exercise has been noted by other researchers (see, for example, Davidson, 1977; Bereiter and Scardamalia, 1983). The free-writing focus, which sometimes includes process approach activities such as brainstorming, although less effective than the previous two focuses, was nonetheless more effective than the 'traditional' focus – which typically does not involve pre-writing activities, multiple drafts and revision. Hillocks concludes that 'free writing and the attendant process orientation are inadequate strategies', proposing the addition of 'procedural knowledge': 'general procedures of the composing process and specific strategies for the production of discourse and the transformation of data for use in writing' (Hillocks, 1987:81).

As there is some evidence to suggest that students tend to transfer L_1 rhetorical patterns into English when writing free compositions (Kaplan, 1967; Connor and McCagg, 1983), it would seem useful to adopt techniques which encourage students to become familiar with L_2 patterns. The 'immediate recall tasks' employed by Connor and McCagg, which involved reading an article in English and then writing a paraphrase of it, seemed to result in the production of L_2 rhetorical patterns with very little sign of L_1 interference. The results of their study suggest that students are influenced by the form of the original article and are thus less likely to transfer L_1 structures to their L_2 prose. The authors conclude that 'there is no indication that the type of transfer observed by Kaplan in free composition, i.e. transfer of culture-specific rhetorical patterns, occurs when non-native English speaking subjects are asked to reconstruct a typical exemplar of English expository prose' (Connor and McCagg, 1983:266).

Research findings also stress the importance of reading. Krashen (1978) claims that extensive reading is actually more useful than a lot of writing practice, and numerous other researchers (Eschholz, 1980; Murray 1968; Widdowson, 1978) have emphasised the significance of the reading-writing link. It is interesting that this aspect of research has managed to bridge the theory-practice gap:

> It is interesting that in spoken communication there is a significant relationship between producing speech and understanding speech. Why not adopt a similar approach with written communication? The writer utilizes syntactic, semantic, discoursal and logical devices to encode the message in the form of a written text. The reader must use the same devices to interpret that message.
>
> (Dubin and Olshtain, 1980:354)

Comments such as the above are echoed in some writing coursebooks: 'We acknowledge the beneficial effect of wide reading on the ability to write (Hamp-Lyons and Heasley, 1987:139). Moreover, it seems that students themselves have become more aware of the importance of reading (see Sandilands, 1989:45 for examples).

The research suggests that students should be given time to write multiple drafts on assignments. The teacher should respond to each draft with specific suggestions for improvement, rather than the vague comments which are often provided. Students should be asked to write to a 'clearly defined real reader' (Flower, 1981:67) in order to enable them to develop a sense of audience and an awareness of style and register. Zamel (1984:199) suggests that teachers should not be the only readers: 'classroom time should be given over to workshop-type collaborative activities in which students comment and raise questions about each other's writing'. Other researchers (Harp, 1988; Johnson, 1983; Raimes, 1983) stress the importance of this type of collaboration.

Teachers should allow time for a variety of writing exercises in class (Zamel, 1984). They should also allow time for correcting and marking (Celce-Murcia, 1988; Johnson, 1988; Rowe, 1982), paying more attention to content than to surface-level errors. If they fail to do so, students will see revision merely as an opportunity to correct local errors, rather than a chance to focus on producing more meaningful texts (Rose, 1983). Harris (1982) notes that by watching students write in class, teachers may be able to discover where they encounter difficulties; for example, too much attention to local errors may interrupt a student's train of thought and hinder them from writing a cohesive text. Zamel, in a comprehensive review of composition research and pedagogy, concludes that 'a process approach provides us with valuable information about our students' knowledge and needs and better insures, to return again to Krashen's (1978) terminology, that teacher input and student intake are more closely aligned' (Zamel, 1984:204).

There is a growing body of evidence to suggest that the use of word processors may enable students to improve their writing skills. Piper (1987:125), after encouraging her students to use word processors during writing classes, concludes that 'through its capacity to engage learners ... more closely in the activity of writing, and by motivating them to write more, and better, the word processor might bring that ideal [improved writing skills] closer to reality'. In order to investigate her students' reactions to using word processors, she asked them to fill in a questionnaire; the response led her to comment that 'in their answers, students gave various reasons for liking word processors, such as its being a useful skill in itself, a modern way of writing, and a help in motivating them to improve their written English' (ibid:122). Kerr and her students found computers useful when working on textual cohesion and organisation of discourse. After using 'Storyboard' (a textual reconstruction exercise) she concluded that 'this computer task is an excellent example of a process-oriented method. The text eventually retrieved is less important than the half-hour spent reconstructing it' (Kerr, 1985:166). As personal computers become more commonly available, more teachers will be able to consider using them during writing classes.

7. A compromise

Although a great deal of research has been done, the often conflicting results and implications make it clear that much more is required. Kantor (1984) notes that there are gaps in the body of research available to us, gaps which must be filled in order to obtain a more comprehensive understanding of composition:

What has been lacking in many composition studies is a picture of the educational context: the conditions under which students write; the methods and style of teachers; the personalities, attitudes, and learning processes of students; and the many interactions among these variables. Composition teaching is a multidimensional phenomenon, one which requires a research methodology that will account for its complexity.

(Kantor, 1984:72)

In the end, given the variety of approaches available and the number of variables in each teaching situation, it would seem best to opt for the 'eclectic approach' advocated by Rivers (1981), providing of course that teachers make principled and informed choices. As Arndt (1987:264) observes: 'it seems unreasonable to suppose that there should be one best way to teach writing in view of the greatly differing needs of individual writers'. Clearly, no one approach is comprehensive enough, just as, in a more general sense, no one method of language teaching is comprehensive enough to be used to the exclusion of all others. Stern (1983:497) criticises twentieth-century language teaching for being 'too broad and ill-defined in some respects, and in others not comprehensive enough', a criticism which could also be directed at individual approaches to writing skills.

Bibliography

Arndt, V. 1987. 'Six writers in search of texts: A protocol based study of L_1 and L_2 writing', *ELT Journal* 41/4, pp. 257-267.

Arnold, J. and Harmer, J. 1978. *Advanced Writing Skills*. London: Longman.

Bereiter, C. and Scardamalia, M. 1983. 'Does learning to write have to be difficult?', in Freedman *et al.* (1983), pp. 20-33.

Brière, Eugene J. 1966. 'Quantity before quality in second language composition', *Language Learning* 16/3 and 16/4, pp. 141-152.

Byrne, D. 1979. *Teaching Writing*. London: Heinemann.

Celce-Murcia, M. 1988. 'Holistic approaches to correcting grammatical errors', *Perspectives* (TESOL-Italy), 14/1, pp. 27-34.

Connor, U. and McCagg, P. 1983. 'Cross-cultural differences and perceived quality in written paraphrases of English expository prose', *Applied Linguistics* 4/3, pp. 259-268.

Corder, S.P. 1967. 'The significance of learners' errors', *IRAL*, 5, pp. 161-170.

Davidson, D.M. 1977. 'Sentence-combining in an ESL writing programme', *Journal of Basic Writing* 3, pp. 49-62.

Dubin, F. and Olshtain, E. 1980. 'The interface of writing and reading', *TESOL Quarterly* 14/3, pp. 353-363.

Emig, J. 1971. *The Composing Process of Twelfth Graders*, NCRTE Research Report No. 13. Urbana, Ill.: National Council of Teachers of English.

Eschholz, Paul A. 1980. 'The prose models approach: Using products in the process', in Donovan, T.R. and McLelland, B. (eds), *Eight Approaches to Teaching Composition*. Urbana, Ill.: National Council of Teachers of English.

Flower, L. 1981. *Problem-Solving Strategies for Writing*. New York: Harcourt Brace Jovanovich, Inc..

Flower, L. and Hayes, J.R. 1980. 'The cognition of discovery: Defining a rhetorical problem', *College Composition and Communication* 31/2, pp. 21-32.

Flower, L. and Hayes, J.R. 1981. 'A cognitive process theory of writing', *College Composing and Communication* 32/4, pp. 365-387.

Freedman, A., Pringle, I. and Yalden, J. (eds), *Learning to Write: First Language/Second Language*. London: Longman.

Hairston, M. 1982. 'The winds of change: Thomas Kuhn and the revolution in the teaching of writing', *College Composition and Communication* 33/1, pp. 76-88.

Hamp-Lyons, L. 1988. 'The product before: Task-related influences on the writer', in Robinson, P. (ed), *Academic Writing: Process and Product* (ELT Documents series). Oxford: MEP and the British Council, pp. 35-46.

Hamp-Lyons, L. and Heasley, B. 1987. *Study Writing*. Cambridge: Cambridge University Press.

Harris, M. 1982. 'Individualised diagnosis: Searching for causes, not symptoms of writing deficiencies', in Harris, M. (ed), *Tutoring Writing*. Glenview, Ill.: Scott, Foresman, pp. 53-65.

Harp, B. 1988. 'Why aren't you using peer editing?', *The Reading Teacher* April 1988, pp. 828-830.

Hedge, T. 1983. *Pen to Paper*. Walton-on-Thames: Nelson.

Hedge, T. 1988. *Writing* (Resource Books for Teachers series). Oxford: Oxford University Press.

Hillocks, G. 1987. 'Synthesis of research on teaching writing', *Education Research* May 1987, pp. 71-82.

Horowitz, D. 1986. What professors actually require: Academic tasks for the ESL classroom', *TESOL Quarterly* 20/3, pp. 445-462.

Hughey, J.B. *et al.* 1983. *Teaching ESL Composition: Principles and Techniques*. Rowley, Mass.: Newbury House.

Jacobs, G. 1987. 'First experience with peer feedback on composition: Student and teacher reaction', *System* 15/3, pp. 325-333.

Johnson, K. 1983. 'Communicative writing practice and Aristotelian rhetoric', in Freedman *et al.* (1983), pp. 247-257.

Johnson, K. 1988. 'Mistake correction', *ELT Journal* 42/2, pp. 89-96.

Kantor, K. 1984. 'Classroom contexts and the development of writing institutions: An ethnographic case study', in Beach, D. and Bridwell, L., *New Directions in Composition Research*. New York: The Guildford Press, pp. 72-94.

Kaplan, R. 1967. 'Contrastive rhetoric and the teaching of composition', *TESOL Quarterly* 1/3, pp. 10-16.

Kerr, Laura 1985. 'Salvaging a disaster: Two lessons with computers', *ELT Journal* 39/3, pp. 162-166.

Krashen, S.D. 1978. 'The monitor model for adult second language performance', in Burt, M. *et al.* (eds), *Viewpoints on English as a Second Language*. New York: Regents, pp. 152-161.

Krashen, S.D. 1984. *Writing Research, Theory and Applications*. Oxford: Pergamon Institute of English.

Lay, N.D.S. 1982. 'Composing processes of adult ESL learners: A case study' (Research note), *TESOL Quarterly* 16/3, p. 406.

Murray, Donald M. 1968. *A Writer Teaches Writing*. Boston: Houghton Mifflin Company.

O'Driscoll, James. 1984. *Advanced Writing Skills*. Harmondsworth: Penguin.

Perl, S. 1979. 'The composing processes of unskilled college writers', *Research in the Teaching of English* 13/4, pp. 317-336.

Piper, A. 1987. 'Helping learners to write: A role for the word processor', *ELT Journal* 41/2, pp. 119-125.

Raimes, A. 1983. *Techniques in Teaching Writing*. New York: Oxford University Press.

Raimes, A. 1985. 'What unskilled ESL students do when they write: A classroom study in composing', *TESOL Quarterly* 19/2, pp. 229-258.

Rivers, W. 1981. *Teaching Foreign Language Skills*. Chicago: University of Chicago Press.

Rose, M. 1983. 'Remedial writing courses: A critique and a proposal', *College English* 45/2, pp. 109-128.

Rowe, T. 1982. 'Thinking twice about correcting', *Lingua e Nuova Didattica*, 11/2, pp. 17-19.

Sandilands, B. 1989. *Developing Writing Skills in the Italian University EFL Programme: A Case Study*. Unpublished M.A. TEFL dissertation, Centre for Applied Language Studies, University of Reading.

Shaugnessy, Mina 1977. *Errors and Expectations: A Guide for the Teacher of Basic Writing*. New York: Oxford University Press.

Sommers, N. 1981. Revision Strategies of student writers and experienced adult writers', *College Composition and Communication* 32/4, pp. 378-388.

Stern, H.H. 1983. *Fundamental Concepts of Language Teaching*. Oxford: Oxford University Press.

Taylor, B.P. 1981. 'Content and written form: A two-way street', *TESOL Quarterly* 15, pp. 5-13.

Watson, C. 1982. 'The use and abuse of models in the ESL writing class', *TESOL Quarterly* 16/1, pp. 5-13.

White, R.V. 1987. *Writing (Advanced)* (Oxford Supplementary Skills series). Oxford: Oxford University Press.

Widdowson, H. 1983. 'New starts and different kinds of failure', in Freedman *et al.* (1983), pp. 34-47.

Zamel, V. 1982. 'Writing: The process of discovering meaning', *TESOL Quarterly*, 16/2, pp. 195-209.

Zamel, V. 1983. 'The composing processes of six advanced ESL students: Six case studies', *TESOL Quarterly* 17/2, pp. 165-185.

Zamel, V. 1984. 'In search of the key: Research and practice in composition', in *On TESOL '83: The Question of Control*. Washington, D.C.: TESOL.

Zamel, V. 1987. 'Recent research on writing pedagogy', *TESOL Quarterly* 21/4, pp. 699-715.

Writing Activities and Text Production in TEFL

Althea Ryan & Hans Arndt

1. Introduction

There is no simple relationship between the writing activities of the English lesson on the one hand, and the acquisition of writing competence in English on the other.

Full writing competence implies the ability to produce a range of types of written text for a range of different situations. This corresponds to the 'communicative competence' which is increasingly advocated for foreign language teaching in general, but is most often implemented in the teaching of the spoken language, its goals defined in terms of the ability to handle a variety of speech situations, such as requesting, promising, apologizing, and so on. For the sake of brevity we shall refer to 'full communicative writing competence' as *text competence.*

Most often the writing exercises used in second language teaching are designed to teach grammatical competence, often referred to as 'code competence' to include spelling and punctuation (in spoken language pronunciation and prosody), as well as syntax and morphology. Code competence is essential, but it is only part of text competence; as it is part of dialogue competence, or indeed of any language user competence.

In the following we shall argue why – at an intermediate or advanced level – code competence is not enough, and we shall suggest what other components should be included in writing teaching. Our main purpose, however, is to demonstrate a didactic approach that may train several – in particular communicative – components of text competence, without resorting to excessive theoretical explanation.

2.1. The goals of writing activities

We may distinguish at least three types of goal in educational writing activities: code training (or testing), content control, and the acquisition of text competence.

Code training is typically the goal of the first writing exercises language students are presented with (such as blank-filling, translations, and sentence transformations). It is aimed at improvement of the students' use of grammar and vocabulary in general, and it is often accompanied by rule-teaching (though it need not be).

Content control is the goal of the type of writing activities that are used to test students' knowledge of areas other than language use, such as literature, culture, history, geography, etc.[1] Clearly the control is exerted by the teacher, and the writing activity is used for testing, not training.

Both code training and content control lead to pedagogical types of writing, where the important thing is to 'get it right', i.e. to work out what the teacher expects, and then write accordingly.

The most comprehensive, but also most abstract goal of writing activities is *the acquisition of text competence*. To acquire text competence involves learning to *determine* the situation, i.e. to determine why you are writing and who for. And on this basis to *decide* on form, i.e. on what content you want to select for your message, and how you want to formulate it.

2.2. Situational determination and formal decisions.

The writing situation has to be *determined,* because in the real world – once you have decided that you want to write – the *purpose* and the *reader* are given. You do not normally sit down to write, purely and simply; you write to someone (a friend or acquaintance, an employer or employee, etc.) in order to convey a message, i.e. to tell them something, or to get them to do something, or just to keep in touch.[2]

On the other hand, content selection and formulation have to be *decided,* because – again in the real world – once you have determined the situation, there are a number of ways in which you can express your message. Hence, learning text competence involves learning to decide on what *text content* to include for your particular purpose and reader, as well as how best to match your *formulation* to the requirements of the content selected, the purpose, and the reader.

The distinction between determination and decision may be less significant in educational than in 'real' communicative writing, in that the challenge for the language teacher is to be able to ensure variety in both respects. Nevertheless it is important to note that – in the normal process of writing – choices (determination) of reader and purpose are logically prior to, because they guide, choices (decisions) as to content and form.

The teacher's role in writing activities that are aimed at the acquisition of text competence is significantly different from his role in other pedagogical writing activities, like code training or content control: not to judge between right or wrong, but to advise on the suitability of decisions on the basis of determinations. There may be more or less appropriate choices (and there may be some distinctly infelicitous ones), but there is no one correct solution.

2.3. Code and communication

Advocates of communicative language teaching have occasionally been accused of a cavalier attitude to code form. And indeed accuracy and fluency in oral proficiency may – at certain stages in the acquisition of a foreign language – be seen as opposite ends of a scale.

To justify careful consideration of both ends of that scale, we may suggest an analogy with first language acquisition. It is generally acknowledged that when babies babble, they are not engaging in a meaningless activity, they are practising the use of their articulatory organs. However, it would be odd, to say the least, to urge a toddler to go on babbling in order to perfect his speech sounds, at a stage when he is able to use them (albeit phonologically imperfectly) to produce real utterances.

No one ever suggested such a perverse procedure for the 'teaching' of first language phonology. Babies are too sweet, and their first steps on the road towards mastery of their native language altogether too mysterious, for anyone to have seriously considered meddling.[3]

If this analogy is accepted, the conclusion for foreign language teaching is that at any stage students should be encouraged to use whatever code competence they have, to try to communicate, rather than keep silent till their code mastery is perfect. This conclusion is quite generally agreed on, even though teaching practice may not always remember to be encouraging.

In foreign language writing there is a somewhat different relation between code and communication. Since writing leaves time for consideration, 'fluency' is less important. And demands for code accuracy need not hamper communication, though they may diminish the speed of the writing process. In fact, familiarity with the finer points of the code (and skilful use of some of the basic ones) may significantly improve communicative efficiency in writing. The important point, however, is that an exclusive focus on code accuracy in evaluation is bound to hamper the students' realization of the communicative (situational) aspects of their writing.

2.4. Code and communication in text competence

At the early stages of foreign language learning, 'code' means the same as in cryptography: an alien form of expression that has to 'broken'. At a more advanced stage, code knowledge is more profitably considered as a means of expression – a tool that will help you learn 'how to mean' (cf. Halliday, 1975).[4]

Clearly some elements in the code are more or less invariable. You need a basic vocabulary, with its inflectional and derivational morphology as well as spelling, and you need a range of possible clause structures. The acquisition of these elements constitutes 'breaking the code'.

But once you have broken the code, and certainly at the stage when communicative writing becomes relevant as an element in the syllabus (the time when this stage occurs varies with student age and learning purpose), you keep running into alternatives: i.e. near-synonymous words, expressions, or clause structures.

Such alternative formulations, which 'mean the same', are often seen by foreign language students as perversities ('Foreigners!') which have been built into the code to make it less accessible. It is part of the teacher's task to help students to realize that the infinite variety allowed in grammar and vocabulary is what makes language expressive (cf. Arndt, 1989).

2.5. Formulation choices

The choices (decisions) that have to be made in order to make language maximally expressive pertain to (1) grammatical structure and vocabulary, (2) textual structure or coherence, and (3) content selection.

Grammatical structure and vocabulary is of course never free in the sense that anything goes. What you want to say does in most cases circumscribe your choice of expression (the exception is the conversational vacuum where any noise is better than silence – but this is minimally relevant for writing). Nevertheless the alternatives[5] are probably wider than is generally recognized, and certainly wider than foreign language students realize. An example, involving sentence structure, ellipsis, and pronominal reference, will show that the alternatives we are talking about do not necessarily presuppose a high degree of code sophistication:

(1) Peter went to see the manager, and he told him that he wasn't doing his job properly.

(2) Peter went to see the manager, who told him that he wasn't doing his job properly.

(3) Peter went to see the manager, and told him that he wasn't doing his job properly.

Situation and context (i.e. reader expectations) will usually disambiguate (1) as either (2) or (3). But the prudent writer will make sure that there is as little of that kind of ambiguity as possible. The important thing to note, however, is that the three examples are all grammatically correct, yet – simple as they are – significantly different in communicative potential.

A rather more striking example of expression variation is the following:

(4) that government of the people, by the people, for the people, shall not perish from this earth.

(5) that people will go on being governed by themselves, and for their own benefit, in at least one place on earth.

Lincoln's famous nominalization (4) is a somewhat more demanding, but clearly also a far more elegant alternative than the straightforwardly pedestrian (5).

Textual coherence is less frequently focal in language teaching exercises than grammatical structure, but it is of paramount importance in text competence. The decisions to be made here are partly global structure (what sections is this text naturally going to be divided into?), and partly local coherence (how is the current sentence related to the next and to the previous one?). These kind of choices may be subsumed under a more comprehensive 'choice of text type' (or format, or genre).

Textual coherence is content organization, but also manifests itself formally in what have been called 'cohesive devices': sentence structure, punctuation, layout, and conjunctions and conjunctive expressions. For instance, the expressions

(6) Once upon a time

(7) Consequently

(8) Yours very sincerely,

would indicate both different text types and different parts of the text. The essential point here is that such indicators form a 'reader's guide' to text structure, and that their use enforces an awareness of text structure.

Content selection is difficult for many students because they have so often been exposed to writing for 'content control'. Their natural assumption is that the idea with a text is to put in as much as they can possibly remember about the topic. Once they have been familiarized with the idea of writing for a particular readership with a particular purpose, the notion of content selection becomes meaningful. It is significant that in terms of the distinction between situational determination and formal decision, content selection is categorized under the latter, as an aspect of text form.

2.6. Product and process

Decisions on formulation, made on the basis of a determination of the situational factors, suggest a consideration of the text as formulated product. However, no experienced writer would maintain that a finished text springs to mind after due consideration of situational factors. For teaching purposes in particular, it is useful to divide the production process into at least four phases, each focusing on specific aspects of the text.

In the *prewriting phase* the author determines the situation and makes preliminary decisions on global structure and content selection. In other words he plans what he wants to say to whom and how.

In the *writing phase* he starts performing, providing himself, as he goes along, with tentative formulations of successive text passages.

The *revision phase* may be preceded by a response phase, in which other students (or the teacher) respond to the results of the writing phase. But the important aspect of revision is to consider the suitability of the formulations made in the writing phase, relative to the choices made in the prewriting phase. And of course to revise accordingly.

In the *editing phase* the result is polished in terms of grammatical structure, vocabulary, and cohesive devices. Focus here is on code correctness, but considerations of alternatives will be important as well. (It is worth noting that in spite of the phases any consideration may intrude itself at any stage.)

2.7. Principles and application

The ramifications of teaching communicative writing skills have been treated elsewhere (Ryan and Arndt, 1989; cf. also Kinneavy, 1983; Lindeberg, 1985; Wikborg, 1985; Evensen, 1985; Björk, 1985; Zamel, 1987; Thomas, 1987; and Hansen, 1990). What we would like to do in the following is to illustrate approaches and techniques in teaching writing, by going through two examples of text manipulation.

The use of actual texts in the teaching of communicative writing skills is beneficial in at least two ways: it allows the exploitation of receptive text analysis as a resource in text production; and it facilitates an understanding of the significance of the revision phase in the production process. The use of the term 'manipulation' (with its affective connotations) in this connection is not fortuitous: the question is, as Humpty-Dumpty so aptly formulated it, who is to be master.

3.0. Approaches and techniques

Once you start breaking down text competence into its component parts, it appears that there is a bewildering range of tasks that the writer has to perform, or aspects to take into account, either simultaneously or consecutively.[6] However, the most appropriate way to teach text competence is not likely to be by way of theoretical insight into each of the components. It might be concluded, then, that the way to text competence goes through composition exercises, i.e. that we teach our students text competence simply by asking them to write texts.[7]

There are several reasons why this 'holistic' type of teaching is not always the most appropriate one (and certainly should not be the only one). First of all, though it may be the teacher's easy option, it leaves the student to find his own way through the bewilderment. By focusing exclusively on the form of the complete finished product, pretending that situation and process do not need specific attention, we leave the students to grapple with all the activities, aspects, or components at the same time. Thus the holistic type of teaching is a violation of the sound principle of education that complex knowledge or competence should be taught in manageable chunks. Holistic teaching provides no easy access to discussing components or steps in the process which the student may need to improve.

A second problem is that without a consideration of situation, there are no criteria by which to evaluate the success of the product, except linguistic correctness and possibly some traditional notions (more often taught by implication than by explanation) about the type of text format that is suitable for the (pedagogical) context. However, the guiding principle for all three types of formulation choice (code, coherence, and content) is that no decision can be made without a prior determination of situation. Without that, any grammatically acceptable alternative may be as good as another. In other words, without explicit situation determination you may be able to suggest how to improve the student text, but not to explain why.

A third – related – problem is that it is unfair to ask anybody to produce texts without telling them what type of text to produce. Partly the (implicit) notion of 'pedagogically suitable text form' tends to hide the variety of possible text types, and is likely to be a source of bewilderment in the 'after life' (e.g. in higher education or in the job market). And partly the teacher is not a very good exemplary recipient – he is far too likely to be looking for particular oversights in editing – when any text production requires an awareness of a specific type of reader.

Finally, it is quite possible to design exercises to teach certain elements of text competence (just as certain grammar exercises teach certain elements of code competence). Fortunately most teachers are aware of this, and a range of teaching materials adopt other routes to text competence. Our aim here is to demonstrate some principles for the design of writing tasks, which would allow the individual teacher to devise his own writing syllabus according to the goal of his teaching and the immediate pedagogical requirements.

3.1. Controlled writing

The holistic writing task suggested in section 3.0 represents one end of a scale from free to controlled writing tasks, where the other end would be a tightly controlled task, such as dictation or translation. In between there are several ways of controlling, or perhaps rather focusing, particular aspects of text competence.

In the following we shall describe an approach which will allow us to focus on aspects of the match between formulation and situation, and at the same time on the revision phase, where this match is checked and refined more concentratedly than in any other phase. In order to reach this phase you are normally forced to go through prewriting and writing first; but there is a short-cut, namely the use of already existing texts, which offers other benefits as well.

First of all you may demonstrate text competence through an analysis of authentic texts (and not primarily literary ones), which focuses particularly on such features of the written text as the writer can be seen to have employed in order to reach his reader and to accomplish his purpose; or in our terms: to match text formulation with text situation. This kind of analysis will help build up an understanding of the requirements of writing, genre and style.

In order to make this understanding productive, almost any text may further be used either as a model, or as a source text for revision. If it is to be used as a model, all you have to do is to change the topic; in other words you ask the students to write a text for a similar audience and with a similar purpose, but on a different topic. This use presupposes, first, that the text is a good one of its kind (i.e. one you consider worthy of emulation); second, that its readership and purpose are within the scope of the students' experience or imagination.

On the other hand, to use a text as a source text for revision, you may choose a text that is atypical of its kind, or perhaps – in your opinion – even flawed (for instance from among the products of a previous group of students, without identifying the individual author of course); after a discussion of atypical features or flaws, the students can then be asked to revise accordingly.

However, you may find the task of finding atypical texts onerous, or flaws unsuitable for a teaching context. And so, alternatively, you may pick out for revision one situational factor in a model text (such as readership age or informative purpose), discuss the ways in which this factor manifests itself in formulation, and then ask the students to revise in accordance with a specific change of the factor (like changing the readership from expert to lay, or changing the purpose from informative to persuasive, and so on).

Conversely, you may specify a change of text form (such as longer/shorter sentences, more/fewer expressions of modality, and so on). And then initiate a discussion of the situational change this reformulation may have occasioned, and perhaps what other formulation changes would naturally go with that.

To sum up, by choosing texts of different types, analyzing them to determine how their situation is reflected in their formulation, and then manipulating aspects of either situation or formulation, you may build up step by step the competence required for text production. This idea will become clearer in the exemplification.

4. Example 1: Revision of a typical text

(9a) **Original text**

Interviewer: How does Britain connect to Europe these days?
Margaret Thatcher: [1]One is very happy if we can in Europe act more coherently together, [2]but not by merging our sovereignty. [3]That is artificial and it will not work. [4]People are proud of their national identity. [5]Just look at East Europe now. [6]Or just look at communism. [7]That was going to be the answer. [8]That was going to overcome all things like national identity, differences, what have you. [9]Of course it did not. [10]It merely suppressed them. [11]You have to identify with something closer than the new world order or human rights. [12]You have to identify with some- -thing which has been part of your life, part of your experience, your memory, your ceremony, your culture. [Extract from NEWSWEEK, Oct. 15, 1990, p.10; numbers of sentences/propositions have been added.]

It may be easiest in this case to look at form relative to situation first. Being an interview, the text is an atypical written text. It has a complex recipient – primarily the journalist who records, ultimately the reader of the magazine. The text form exhibits a number of features typical of spoken, rather than written language.

These features are, for instance: the extreme brevity of many sentences (cf. 3-7, 9-10); the use of syntactic repetition to create coherence (cf. 5-6, 7-8, 11-12); the interactive aspect (and referential ambiguity) evident in the use of personal pronouns (e.g. *one* and *we* in [1], *our* in [2], *you(r)* in [8, 11, 12]); and the use of colloquial expressions rather than more carefully worded ones (such as *be very happy* and *act ... together* in [1], *just look* in [5, 6], *was going to* in [7, 8], *you have to* in [11, 12]).

Without presuming to know how Mrs. Thatcher would express herself in writing, it may nevertheless be possible to suggest a revision from spoken to written language. Whether you want to undertake this exercise by way of illustration (i.e. presenting your own revised version for comparison) or by way of a controlled writing task, depends on the stage of text competence your students have reached. We shall suggest some possible revisions, which would make the text conform to a more formal written style.

In [1] the use of *one* suggests a generalized self: herself as a representative of Britain (as confirmed in the interviewer's question). To *be very happy* (which naturally and colloquially takes a 1st person subject) about a future action *x* of which the subject is a (partial) agent, means, say, to 'be very willing to join in (efforts at) bringing about *x*'. The personal pronoun *we* here means 'Britain and the other European countries'. *Act ... together* means 'co-operate'; and in this connection *more coherently* functions as a positive valuation of the 'cooperation', potentially expressible by a lexical item like 'improve'. Hence a more formal version might be

(9b)   Britain is very willing to join in attempts to improve European cooperation.

In the subsequent text, *our sovereignty* [2] identifies British rather than European 'sovereignties' (the reference of *our* is different from that of *we* in [1]). The notion of sovereignty is immediately re-generalized by *people* [4] and *East Europe* [5] (not only the British are *proud of their national identity* [4]). Similarly, the non-mergeability of British sovereignty is echoed in the non-suppressibility of any *national identity* [8-10]. Altogether this suggests a continuation as follows:

(9c)   but we do not believe in giving up national sovereignty, because that is artificial and will not work.

Obviously this calls for substantiation, which Thatcher is very willing to give – *just look at East Europe* [5] and *just look at communism* [6] (despite the parallel constructions, the latter is a specification of the former rather than a parallel: i.e. 'Just look at East Europe, I mean communism in East Europe'). Moreover, *be the answer* [7] and *overcome* [8] are fairly close textual synonyms (i.e. they are synonymous in this text, not in a general dictionary sense); both suggest a negatively valued object: *differences* [8] (or 'conflicts'), whereas the expression *national identity* [8] (cf. also [4]) matches more naturally with *suppress* [10], which here requires a positively valued object. Altogether we may continue:

(9d)   East European communism, for instance, which was supposed to overcome national differences and conflicts, has simply suppressed national identity.

In this way we switch more easily from 'national sovereignty' and 'differences/conflicts', to 'pride in national identity', which Thatcher goes on to specify in the final section of her answer. A natural written formulation might be the following, which explicates the 'fact' of *national identity,* in contrast to the mirage of international communism:

(9e) The fact is that people are proud of their national identity. They need to identify with something closer than the new world order or human rights, something that is part of their experience, memory, ceremony, or culture.

Together, the revised version looks like this:

(9f) **Revised text**
Britain is very willing to join in attempts to improve European cooperation, but we do not believe in giving up national sovereignty, because that is artificial and will not work. East European communism, for instance, which was supposed to overcome national differences and conflicts, has simply suppressed national identity. The fact is that people are proud of their national identity. They need to identify with something closer than the new world order or human rights, something that is part of their experience, memory, ceremony, or culture.

The task set in order to trigger a revision along these lines is of course a matter of the particular teaching situation. Here are two suggestions:

(10) How could these opinions have been expressed if Mrs. Thatcher had been writing directly to the readers instead of through the medium of the interview with the journalist? [This task focuses primarily on situation.]

(11) Change the formulation of the text from spoken to written. Pay particular attention to sentence length, repetition, personal pronouns, sequence, and synonyms.
Feel free to change grammatical structure and word classes (e.g. *proud-pride*) and to replace words with more formal synonyms, but remember that Thatcher is a politician talking to her constituency, not a philosopher, and do not change the argumentative position or force, nor the situation in general. [This task focuses more explicitly on the formal changes to be made. But both (10) and (11) would be answered by something like (9f).]

The point of the exercise it to show that there are alternatives, in grammar and text structure, as well as in vocabulary; that these alternatives are tied to the situation; and that it is not a question of choosing between right and wrong (few people would dare to suggest that Thatcher's language is 'wrong' or 'bad'; on the contrary it is very effective, and we would not like to suggest that our version is more expressive).

There are several details in the revised version that might deserve further comment, particularly with regard to sentence structure and coherence. However, we shall deal with only one more problem: Could students who are grappling with the adjustment of their interlanguage to the target language be expected to produce a version like (9f)? The answer is that it is unlikely to be the result of their first attempt at revision; but it is quite possible to limit oneself at first to a revision of, say, sentence length, repetition and pronouns. A result like the following, which takes account of only some of the changes possible, would not seem to be unduly ambitious:

(12) **An alternative version**
Margaret Thatcher: [1]Britain is very happy if the European nations can act more coherently together, [2]but not by merging their sovereignty. [3]That is artificial and it will not work, [4]because people are proud of their national identity. [5]Just look at communism in East Europe now. ([6]) [7]That was going to be the answer [8]which would overcome all things like national identity, differences, and what have you, [9]but of course it merely suppressed them. ([10]) [11]You have to identify with something closer than the new world order or human rights, [12]something which has been part of your life, experience, memory, ceremony, and culture.

5. Example 2: Revision according to situation

In example 1 the situational change was minor, though significant, the formulation changes far more obvious. In example 2 we shall focus more on the features of situation.

(13a) **Original Text**
HOW TO BUY A HEALTHY KITTEN
Examine the kitten closely before buying. The eyes should be clear, not watering excessively, and white skin at corners should not show. Nostrils should be clear, not exuding mucus, a sure sign of incubating health problems. The ears should be clean without excessive dirt or wax-like substance which indicates the presence of mites. Examine the fur by spreading the fur and looking at the skin for sores and scabs indicating fungus condition. Check fur for fleas or flea eggs which look like small black dots. Check kitten's litter pan for signs of diarrhea. [Extract from *Cat Catalog*, New York: Crown Publishers, 1982.]

As in the first example the exercise starts with analysis. We shall not go into detail, just note that both lexis and syntax (and presentation in general) suggest a general reader, not an expert, nor a child. The purpose is a mixture of informative and instructive (regulative); note, for example, syntactic features reminiscent of a recipe.

A first exercise might be a change of lexis to make the text accessible for a child. This does not seem to produce a very interesting result. We change *excessive(ly)* to 'a lot of' or 'too much'; *not exuding* to 'without'; *wax-like substance* to 'wax'; and leave out *incubating* and *condition*. But the text still looks blandly unappealing to a child, which is not surprising, since there is greater stylistic potential in syntactic, semantic, or pragmatic changes. In other words, formulation changes occasioned by situational changes constitute a whole, and however important vocabulary is for the acquisition of a foreign language, it is not enough for the acquisition of text competence.

Hence the second exercise is to change the text so as to make it suitable for an audience of 10-12-year-olds, who are absolutely dying to get hold of a furry little pet. This kind of situational change is well motivated (acquiring a pet is more often a child's idea than an adult's), and it provides wide scope (though within certain situational limits) for changes of syntax and presentation, and selection of content. Finally the variation that is likely to ensue provides ample opportunity for a discussion of appropriateness, especially because the situation is well within the scope of the students' experience or imagination. To illustrate the potential of this exercise we would like to suggest the following version:

(13b) **Revised version**
HOW TO GET A HEALTHY KITTEN
All kittens are lovely, eager to play and simply waiting to be cuddled. But your cat is going to be with you for the next ten or fifteen years. So if you have a choice (and you usually do), you might as well make sure you get one that is healthy and able to live a good life. You *can* check that the kitten you are dying to take home with you is in good condition.
LOOK AT THE EYES. They should be clear, not watering too much, and there shouldn't be any white skin showing at the corners.
LOOK AT THE NOSE. If it isn't clear, but runny, the kitten is not healthy. On the other hand the nose must not be dry and warm, it should be cold and moist.
LOOK AT THE EARS. Too much dirt or wax indicates mites, which is a pest that it can be difficult to get rid of.
LOOK AT THE FUR. Spread it to look for sores or scabs that indicate skin diseases. Fleas or flea eggs show up as little black dots.
Finally check the kitten's litter pan, to make sure it makes firm little piles, not messy ones.

Obviously this is not the only possible solution to the exercise (and so very clearly allows for a consideration of appropriateness and stylistic choice, rather than just correctness), but it does focus syntactic, coherence, and layout changes, to match the change of readership. In order to focus text purpose we might try to change it into a more informative, less regulative, style:

(13c) **An alternative revision**
HOW TO CHECK A CAT FOR DISEASES
If you want to be sure that your cat is in good health, here are some very obvious signs to look for:
A healthy cat has clear eyes, which do not water, and with no white skin showing at the corners.
Her nose is clean, moist, and cold, not runny, nor warm and dry.
Her ears are clean. Dirt or wax indicates mites, which is a pest that it can be difficult to get rid of.

Her skin is without sores or scabs that indicate skin diseases. Fleas or flea eggs show up in the fur as little black dots.

The litter pan reveals your cat's digestion, depending on whether it contains neat firm piles, or messy fluid ones.

With this last version we have switched the situation from 'buying a kitten' to 'checking a cat', as well as changing the purpose from regulative to primarily informative. The main thing here is to observe the changes, with a view to teaching the formulation differences that go with situational change. One major difference between this and the original version is layout, which may serve to emphasize the importance of an aspect that is otherwise not normally given much consideration.

6. Some further suggestions

There is a limit to how much you can use one text for revision. Presumably two revisions will exhaust the students' patience with the subject-matter in hand. However, for the sake of exemplification, we would like to suggest here some other tasks based on the two texts (9a) and (13a). The tasks would be suitable at different stages of writing competence.

The following tasks are only controlled in so far as the text situation is specified and our texts are the starting point. In themselves they do not constitute revision exercises, but an extension into independent text writing on the basis of analysis, discussion and possibly revision activities with the original texts.

(14) Write a short argument (10-20 sentences) from a nationalist to an (unknown and mass) audience of internationalists, the topic is national identity and international cooperation.

[This task might be based on an analysis/discussion of (9a), and possibly a revision task focusing on argumentation and differences between written and spoken formulation. The answer might sound somewhat like (9f), except that Britain would not be the point of departure, though it might provide an example.]

(15) Write a short argument (10-20 sentences), as from an internationalist to a friend who is a nationalist.

[Preparation tasks could well be similar to those in (14). The answer would have to switch some values, as well as the degree of formality and reference to situation; it should result in a more friendly and relaxed style. Hence (15) would be more demanding than (14).]

(16) Write a very short text to be included in a brochure for the general public about buying pets (available at public libraries, pet shops, and from vets). The brochure has several sections, you are to write the paragraph under the heading 'Is it healthy?'.

[This task requires generalization of the factors mentioned in (13a) and a consideration of what kinds of pets people buy. The audience is similar to the one for the original text.]

(17) Write a letter to the Royal Society for the Prevention of Cruelty to Animals (RSPCA) complaining about the condition of the cats and kittens at a cattery you visited a few days ago. You are thinking of buying a Siamese kitten and you responded to an advertisement in your local paper.

[This is quite a difficult task requiring a formal style and the expression of a negative attitude. The emotional aspect (indignation) would provide a good basis for pre-writing discussion: e.g. will the arguments be undermined if you express strong indignation? should one stick to facts and observations only in order to have a stronger effect? can one be formal and emotional at the same time? etc. This task also gives scope for the imagination.]

(18) HOW I GOT MY CAT. Specify your recipient.

[This may occasion a discussion of the type of recipient imaginable for that kind of communication. It may also, compared to the type of text required by the previous tasks, occasion a discussion of the differences between argumentative and narrative styles. Incidentally, if you specify a child as recipient in this task, you may end up with a version that looks very much like the cute little stories in beginners' books.]

7. Conclusion

We have chosen above to demonstrate a teaching technique by means of concrete examples. This should not obscure the general principle, i.e. that text manipulation can be a powerful means in writing teaching.

It is difficult to specify exactly a didactic procedure, because this will depend on the details of the educational situation. But the following may be a natural progression of task types:

A Choose a text and make whatever formal changes (including grammar, coherence, punctuation, and layout) you or your students can think of, without changing the essence of the content.

This first step is to alert students to the infinite variety of grammatically acceptable expressions.

B Compare the various versions you have produced with the original, and discuss how the versions differ in the impressions they make on the reader. Try to distinguish between changes which are compatible with the original situation (reader and purpose) and those which are not. Determine the situation of the original text.

This second step is to teach the students the relationship between formulation and situation, and the way in which the latter restricts the former.

C Choose a text and specify a change of readership and/or purpose. Discuss ensuing changes in formulation (grammar, coherence, punctuation, and layout). If your choice of text and specification of change are right, they will occasion a discussion also of content selection.

This third step is to help training the student's own skill at text manipulation.

D Specify a topic, a reader, and a purpose. Discuss restrictions on content selection and formulation. Write, and resume discussion.

This final type marks the transition from text manipulation to independent, individual text production.

In summary, the general principle is that the learner is made aware of the necessity of considering the communicative situation of a text and making appropriate choices at all levels from content to layout. The focus on choice is made evident both in the methodology and in the tasks set. In analysis and manipulation exercises the learner is made aware of the types of choices to be made, e.g. layout, sentence length, selection and organization of arguments, vocabulary, etc., and a battery of alternatives is built up. At the same time manipulation exercises will train aspects of the writing process, predominantly the mental set involved in actively bringing to mind and considering alternatives.

Independent text production tasks, if they are to provide training rather than testing, presuppose pre-writing and response/revision activities, with consideration of available appropriate and inappropriate choices in the pre-writing activities, and evaluation of the choices made in the response and revision activities. In this the teacher's role becomes more and more advisory, the writing process becomes more important, and the product may go through several drafts. The final draft is ideally one which is regarded by the student (rather than just the teacher) as satisfactory.

The approach we have suggested is by no means revolutionary. Any writer of prose will have had to consider the factors we have presented. What is new, however, is the technique that connects the real writing situation with the educational one. We believe that the connection can make educational writing more interesting, and first attempts at real writing less daunting.

Notes

1. In fact writing for geography, history, etc. also involves communicative, or discourse, skills, but this is not generally recognized, and is often obscured by the way in which such writing products are corrected and evaluated.
2. The idea of situation determination is really quite simple: to make a mental note of purpose and reader; and it would seem to be a superfluous reminder. Yet in much educational and also official writing, the sender seems to take little account of the needs of his or her reader. As far as students are concerned, it is not unlikely that their educational experience, i.e. writing in order to impress someone who is only formally and occupationally interested in what they have to say, has blunted their sense of a communicative situation.
3. For grammar the situation is different. Remedial grammar teaching has in fact been proposed for young speakers of minority dialects who were quite capable of communicating appropriately in situations that were natural for them (cf. Baratz and Baratz, 1972, Labov, 1972).
4. The presupposition here is that you have something to 'mean', i.e. that you have a message to communicate to a reader. This is why the determination of purpose and reader is so important for decisions on formulation (use of the code) and content.
5. Alternatives are often considered primarily in terms of synonyms in the vocabulary, but they also include, say, sentence structure and ellipsis, tense and modality, forms of pronominal and nominal reference, etc.
6. This is not really surprising, since there is no reason to suppose that text competence is any less complicated than grammatical code competence, which involves the teaching of a broad range of lexical, morphological and syntactic subskills.
7. Providing as input just a title, like 'Characterize the main character in the short story' or 'What did you do in your summer vacation?'

References

Arndt, Hans. 1989. 'Expressiv Grammatik', *Hermes* 2, Handelshøjskolen i Aarhus, pp. 109-126.

Baratz, Stephen S. and Baratz, Joan C. 1972. 'Early childhood intervention: the social science base of institutional racism', in *Language in Education: A Source Book*. London: Routledge and Kegan Paul, The Open University Press, pp. 188-197.

Björk, Lennart. 1985. 'TUAP and the teaching of writing in Sweden', in Enkvist (1985), pp. 27-38.

Enkvist, Nils Erik (ed.). 1985. *Coherence and Composition: A Symposium*. Åbo Akademi.

Evensen, Lars Sigfred (ed.). 1985. *Nordwrite Reports I*. TRANS II, Universitetet i Trondheim.

Freedman, Aviva, Pringle, Ian and Yalden, Janice (eds.). 1983. *Learning to Write: First Language/Second Language*. London: Longman.

Halliday, M.A.K.. 1975. *Learning How to Mean*. London: Edward Arnold.

Hansen, Elisabeth. 1990. 'Prodata – tendenser og udviklinger i børns skriftsprog', in Kunø, Mette and Larsen, Erik Vive (red.), *3. møde om udforskningen af dansk sprog*. Aarhus, pp. 111-125.

Kinneavy, James L. 1983. 'A pluralistic synthesis of four contemporary models for teaching composition', in Freedman et al. (1983), pp. 121-138.

Labov, W. 1972. 'The logic of nonstandard English', in *Language in Education: A Source Book*. London: Routledge and Kegan Paul, The Open University Press, pp. 198-212.

Lindeberg, Ann-Charlotte. 1985. 'Functional role analysis applied to narrative and non-narrative student essays in EFL', in Evensen (1985), pp. 26-45.

Ryan, Althea and Arndt, Hans. 1989. 'Fremmedsproglig produktion – at skrive', in Kasper, G. and Wagner, J., *Grundbog i Fremmedsprogspædagogik*. Copenhagen: Gyldendal, pp. 48-61.

Thomas, Sharon. 1987. *A New Paradigm for Teaching English: Writing as a Process*. PEO (Prepublications of the English Department of Odense University), 41.

Wikborg, Eleanor. 1985. 'Types of coherence breaks in university student writing', in Enkvist (1985), pp. 93-133.

Zamel, Vivian. 1987. 'Recent research on writing pedagogy', *TESOL Quarterly* 21/4, pp. 697-715.

Testing and Teaching Foreign Language Writing Skills at University Level

Shirley Larsen

It might seem like putting the cart before the horse to put testing before teaching, but within any institutionalised system of teaching, there is a considerable washback effect from examinations upon what goes on in the classroom. This is especially true of the teaching of writing skills at advanced level, where the tendency is to gear the day-to-day work towards the examination that students will be sitting at the end of that particular course. Indeed, at Danish universities students not only expect to be told the examination rules and requirements right from the start, they also, and this seems legitimate, expect the teaching to be directly related to the examination in the sense that whatever they are asked to do should reflect the aims and requirements of the examination itself.

1. Testing and teaching at the University of Aarhus

In the course of the past twenty years, the testing and teaching of writing skills in English have undergone considerable change at the University of Aarhus in Denmark, as the following three types of examination paper, set at ten-year intervals, will illustrate. In each case, the examination was sat at the end of two years' full-time study of English, these two years constituting Part I of a four-year degree course.

In 1971, the examination comprised a translation from Danish into English. The candidates were required to translate a 350-word Danish text, which could be taken from a work of fiction or non-fiction, including serious newspaper articles. No dictionaries or aids of any kind were allowed. The examination lasted three hours.

In 1981, the examination comprised a 250-word summary in English of a Danish article of about 1,200 words; a translation into English of a given passage of approximately 250 words taken from the same article; and an essay in English, of the candidate's own choice, on the theme or a particular aspect of the article. No dictionaries or aids of any kind were allowed. The examination lasted six hours. In the summer of 1981 the two articles that the candidates had to choose between dealt with the role of old people in society in the one case, and problems of communication arising from the overuse of academic Danish in the other. Essay topics were suggested (although the candidates were free to choose their own).

In 1991, the examination lasted four hours, and the candidates were allowed dictionaries and any other kind of aid they considered relevant. They were required to answer the following two questions:

(1) Read through Text 1, which is a short article from a Danish information sheet on ERASMUS (the EC scheme promoting exchanges between University students and staff in the countries of the European Community).

The interview with Niels Hybel took place after he had completed his month's teaching at the University of Lancaster. You are to imagine that he was interviewed by a reporter from Lancaster University's monthly newspaper towards the end of his stay in Lancaster. You are to rewrite (i.e. translate/transform) the Danish interview in English in such a way that it is suitable for readers of the English publication. You will find that you have to make some changes and possibly add some information about Danish universities. You may restructure the text if you wish.

You are also to write brief comments on your translation/transformation (e.g. pointing out any changes you found it necessary to make, and any specific translation problems you may have encountered).

(2) Text 2 consists of three short extracts from a book entitled *The Birds of Britain and Northern Europe*.

Imagine that you are the writer of a weekly wildlife column for a local newspaper. The newspaper circulates in a rural part of Suffolk, a county in south-eastern England. There are many villages, isolated houses and farms in this area. The column is entitled 'The Wildlife Around You'.

This is the time of year when birds are raising their young, and this week you have decided to write about owls. Using Text 2 as your source of information, write the article for this week. You do not need to include all the information from Text 2 in your article.

In this article it is my intention to focus on the most recent type of examination, its objectives, and its implications for teaching. However, I should also like to comment on the two earlier types, partly because I have been involved in preparing students for these, partly because the lessons that we as teachers learned from them led to the implementation of the present form of examination.

2.1. The translation-based examination

In the 1960s and even later, it seems that writing skills in a foreign language were still primarily taught through the medium of translation in universities throughout Europe, and that translation often constituted the main, if not the only, written test of proficiency in the foreign language. There were, admittedly, obvious advantages in this form of test, particularly from a teaching point of view. Texts could be selected on the basis of the type of structures and vocabulary that the students needed to practise and develop; the marking load was relatively light, as students tended to make the same kinds of mistake; the translation itself formed the basis of the classroom work and led on to the discussion of, for instance, various grammar points and synonyms. Everybody, students and teacher alike, had a sense of accomplishment at the end of the class: a text had been thoroughly discussed from a contrastive point of view and a number of grammatical, structural and lexical points had been covered. Looking back, however, I realise that there was at least one major failing in my teaching, and that is that it was to a large extent mistake-oriented. As at this stage of their studies students frequently make a variety of mistakes, it made good sense to explain these in some detail, but they were very often, of course, mistakes that were generated in particular by the Danish text and the tendency of the students to translate directly. The question is whether the same mistakes would necessarily have occurred in free production. Another question is whether translation in fact helped students to improve their writing skills in general. In other words, the question was whether they transferred what they were supposed to learn from translating to the free production of English in other disciplines, where they were indeed expected to be able to write correct and idiomatic English, too. My main objection to translation, which is a highly useful skill and a valuable contrastive exercise, was that we tended to look at English through the medium of Danish instead of focussing primarily on the English language and its resources, which is probably what students need to do at this level.

2.2. The summary plus translation plus essay examination

When a completely new degree course was introduced in 1974, it was decided that more emphasis should be placed on the teaching of language proficiency than hitherto, and accordingly that writing skills should be tested in a variety of ways. The new examination, in which students were required to translate, to summarise, and to write an essay, tested the students in various areas, moving as it did from bound production to completely free production. It was felt that the translation tested the ability to produce certain structures in

English, to render lexical items accurately and to reproduce a given style. The summary tested the ability to produce a coherent, cohesive and concise text, written in accurate and idiomatic English. It was free to the extent that the students could choose their own structures and up to a point their own vocabulary. The essay was again expected to be coherent and cohesive, but here the students could choose their own style, opinions and approach.

My own objection was, however, that the examination still forced us to work with Danish texts as the starting-point. Admittedly, as students attended classes for two years before sitting the examination, it was possible to use English texts for the purpose of summarising and as a basis for essay-writing in the initial stages. It was also possible to use other types of exercise as a preparation for both these skills. But there was one major problem, and that was that these writing exercises were not aimed at a particular audience and they had no particular purpose. The students found the summary exercise extremely difficult and often frustrating, simply because they had to confine themselves to a given word-count. This meant that they found themselves spending time on paring down the text to the required number of words. It sometimes meant that a good, idiomatic expression had to be discarded in favour of a more concise, but less effective, expression. It was often experienced, then, as a kind of strait-jacket. The essay was not popular either. Students frequently found it hard to write about a given topic (especially if it was a topic that did not appeal to them – and no single topic appeals to everyone), even though we discussed various approaches, styles and essay types, and looked at different models. They felt very much that there was no real purpose in producing these texts; they were purely and simply exercises written for the teacher/examiner. In fact, during the year, it was not possible to get them to write many essays. They preferred to spend their time on the translation and the summary exercises, because these did not require them to express their own opinions.

From the point of view of the teacher, the work-load was decidedly heavier. The summaries in particular generated a wide range of mistakes, and a number of these tended to be individual ones, which had to be corrected and explained individually. The great difficulty with the summary was writing a text that was not only concise, but also coherent and cohesive. Many students were able to restrict themselves to the required number of words, but at the expense of the overall coherence. In the end, most of them did learn to produce acceptable summaries, but it was sometimes a long, slow and rather dreary process, and, in retrospect, I think that the time could more usefully have been spent on other aspects of writing. Again, as with the translation, the summary seemed to lend itself more to a discussion of mistakes and correctness than to an analysis of style and other features of writing. Nevertheless, students did improve their writing skills in general, they developed an awareness of what makes a text cohere and a rudimentary sense of style, and they became reasonably proficient at translating.

2.3. The text transformation examination

The examination was again changed in 1986, once more in connection with a new degree course. The language components became an integrated course, the idea being that the same teacher should, as far as possible, teach not only oral and writing skills, but also the theoretical disciplines, which include theoretical grammar and discourse analysis. The new examination in writing skills is text-based and has been given the rather awkward name 'Text Transformation and Production'. The objective of the new writing course is that students should learn how to produce (by which we also understand translate) a variety of text types, and that the examination should test their ability to produce two or three different types of text. Each text has to be written for a specific audience and for a specific purpose. In addition, the students are required to comment on the various considerations and choices they had to make in the production of at least one of these texts. The ideas of Hans Arndt and Althea Ryan on text transformation, described earlier in this volume (pp. 43-61), were very influential in the design of the new examination.

Since no one can produce a text without having something to write about, some kind of input is necessary. This input takes the form of a text, which the student has to transform, usually quite considerably, in order to produce a different text type, frequently for a different audience and nearly always for a different purpose.

I have to admit that I was initially extremely sceptical about the new examination, particularly because of the implications for teaching. For one thing, I was not certain that I myself was capable of producing the range of text types that the students would be required to produce. In addition, I was, or so I thought, very much aware of the students' linguistic limitations, and did not see that they would be able to meet the new demands. Finally – and this in the event proved to be highly revealing of my own attitude to teaching writing – I was very much afraid that we would be teaching them what I considered superficial skills, and would not be dealing with what I regarded as fundamental, i.e. correctness. To express this slightly differently, I feared that we would be giving the students a superficial acquaintance with various text types at the expense of a solid knowledge of what constitutes grammatically correct and lexically appropriate English. This is not quite so thick-headed as it may sound. No matter what one teaches, there is a limited amount of time available, and I had envisaged that the time that had hitherto been spent on helping students to correct the typical mistakes that Danes make would be considerably reduced in favour of analysing the typical features of different types of text. In other words, my basic approach to writing skills was still mistake-oriented.

Now, this is not a fairy story, and the change of approach has not resulted in students who write impeccable prose on all occasions. But the change of approach has meant that the focus is on something other than mere correctness.

The focus is on the students' ability to produce a text that has a particular effect on a given audience – and if they are able to do this, then the mistakes that they may happen to make tend to be less obtrusive than in the type of largely purposeless writing where there is little else to focus on. The text that they produce has, then, a purpose; and it is the purpose of the text, and the extent to which that purpose is fulfilled, that is central. This does not mean that accuracy is no longer considered important. Obviously a text that is riddled with language mistakes is not going to achieve its aim, as certain types of mistake, or a plethora of mistakes, can most definitely distract the reader. On the other hand, a text that is basically effective, because it makes a point and takes account of the audience, can well contain mistakes that the reader might not even notice, at least at a first reading. The point is that in writing for a purpose, and in considering the needs, demands and composition of a target group, students generally become much more conscious of the language they are using, and of the structure of the text as a whole. As a result, it is usually easier to make them see when their text lacks cohesion or coherence, and to make them aware of the categories of mistake that they typically make.

3. The new approach

As will now be apparent, my original scepticism about the new approach to writing skills was largely unfounded. The new approach works, and, on the whole, works well. I should now like to go into some detail about the different types of text that we attempt to teach, how we actually set about it, and how the new course is perceived by the students themselves.

3.1. Text types

The texts that we expect the students to be able to produce are basically informative, argumentative and/or persuasive. They can be written for the general public, often a relatively educated public, or for a more restricted audience. The styles that we are aiming at are, then, those that most students can cope with, i.e. either relatively formal or neutral (but not highly formal or academic) or relatively informal (but not tabloid newspaper style or intensely personal). The style as such is important: it should not extend the students beyond their own limits. This does not mean that we do not expect the students to be able to produce academic writing in English, but this ability will be fully acquired at a later stage of their studies.

The question is, of course, what types of text the general public, or a more restricted audience, might be expected to read. The range is obviously wide, and what we actually ask the students to produce is determined as much as anything else by expediency and plausibility – and length. Length is an important factor, not least in the day-to-day teaching, as students normally hand in written work every week. It is also important that the students should write the kind of text that they could conceivably (maybe stretching one's imagination a little) be required to produce in their future careers, and that the task we give them seems plausible. So far, our own imaginations as teachers have stretched to include: articles for the general public, such as a news story or a feature article for a non-tabloid newspaper or a non-specialist magazine; feature articles for a specific target group, such as students or businessmen; short articles for a textbook for British or American school children; letters (e.g. to the editor, to a friend, to an employer); leaflets (on a variety of subjects and with very different purposes); reports; items for inclusion in a tourist brochure; instructions/regulations; encyclopaedia entries.

It could be objected that Danish graduates are unlikely to find themselves writing, for instance, encyclopaedia entries in English. It could also be objected that writing newspaper articles is the preserve of the journalist. It is, however, highly likely that they will, depending on the kind of employment they find, be required to produce informative material of various kinds, ranging from factual reports to persuasive material promoting a company and its products. Here it is of interest to note that former students have indeed found that they have been asked to write texts of this nature, mainly in Danish but also in English, and, moreover, that they were expected to create the texts themselves, and not simply translate someone else's work. Yet even though graduates may primarily be required to produce Danish texts, the mere fact that they have considered different formats and different styles in English will have made them aware of the kind of considerations it is necessary to make. They will, in fact, have become sensitive to a wider range of styles and text types than they have been exposed to, because in the course of the teaching they come to realise that it is not only the presence but also the absence of certain features that contribute to a given style and a given type of text. They will have become conscious of the differences between the purpose and structure of, say, a leaflet on the one hand and of an article on the other, and this will have given them a basis for tackling unfamiliar types of text. They will have learned to present facts, briefly and without comment, as in an encyclopaedia, and persuasively or argumentatively, as in certain types of article and letter. Such awareness and skills can potentially be transferred to other situations and other text types, and even to other languages, provided one is aware of the distinctive ways in which different cultures approach such tasks. And what we hope is that a course like ours will sensitize students to language and textuality in general, and not only to one specific language and the textual features that are associated with that language and culture.

3.2. Source material

Before the students can actually begin producing different text types, they need to know something about the features associated with them, and they also need material on which to base their text. We do not normally expect them to find their own information and arguments, as we feel this would be placing an unreasonable burden on them; the writing skills course is, after all, only part, and a fairly small part, of the first two years of their degree course. The input is therefore provided in the form of a text of some kind from which the students are expected to extract the arguments, ideas and/or information needed to produce the new text. The source material provided varies widely from articles to encyclopaedia entries, from formal to informal style. This means that the input can often take the form of a kind of a text that the student will at some time be required to produce, and thus also serves as a kind of model.

In fact, we do not always provide a model text type, partly because we are afraid that a model presented as the model may turn out to be a strait-jacket, partly because a satisfactory authentic model, as opposed to one that we, the teachers, produce ourselves, is not always available. Different text types are, of course, discussed in detail, particularly in the initial stages of teaching, but sometimes the students are thrown in at the deep end, and asked to produce a kind of text that they have not encountered before. The new text type, and its possible features, are first discussed in class, parallels being drawn with texts that have already been dealt with. When the students' work is returned, we often select a few of their efforts, or perhaps extracts from them, such as openings and conclusions, to examine in detail. On other occasions, we work out a text ourselves, and invite the students to criticise it. So while some form of model is not necessarily provided prior to the writing exercise, students are given the opportunity afterwards to see and analyse approaches that differ from their own.

3.3. Writing tasks

For the past three years we have begun the course with letter-writing. My colleague, Tim Caudery, wrote a set of three model letters, the first being a formal letter from a firm of engineering consultants to a car rental company, arranging for a car to be reserved in Australia for one of the consultants; the second, a formal, but friendly, letter from the consultant to the company manager he was to meet in Australia, confirming the details of the visit; the third, again a letter from the consultant to the company manager in Australia confirming the details of the visit, but this time an informal business letter written to an old business friend. The three letters are obviously different as regards layout, the kind of information included, and in particular style. The students are asked to pinpoint both differences and similarities in a short group-work session, after which these features are discussed briefly in class. The task for homework is to rewrite a letter from a bookshop to a customer, and a holiday postcard from a woman to a friend, both of which have been written in totally inappropriate styles. These pieces of correspondence have been dubbed 'Tim's Silly Letters' (see Appendix 1), and silly though they are, they make an admirable starting-point for creating consciousness of style, and a sense of what is relevant and irrelevant information. In their first year at university, students tend to be very unsure of what constitutes formal as opposed to informal style, and although the versions of these two pieces of writing that they produce are a considerable improvement on the originals, very few students manage to write completely convincing texts. The tendency is to mix formal and informal features and to include the kind of information or comment that is inappropriate for the circumstances.

One year, we followed the letter-writing by focussing on factual prose, selecting a short extract from the *Encyclopaedia Britannica* on department stores. We discussed the way in which the text was built up, moving from a brief definition of a department store to a few historical facts, followed by more detailed information about the function of a modern department store, with some comment on its particular advantages. We then asked the students to produce a similar encyclopaedia piece on the Danish *gymnasium* (roughly the equivalent of the English Sixth Form College or the American High School). Here, the students were expected to draw on their own knowledge of the *gymnasium*, but to help them with some of the necessary vocabulary, we gave them a one-page extract from the British Encyclopaedia on secondary education in the Scandinavian countries. This task proved to be far too difficult. The structure of the Danish *gymnasium* is highly complex and they did not know enough about the comparable institutions in Britain or America to know which features needed explaining, or indeed, how to explain these features. The vocabulary represented a problem, as there are often no exact lexical equivalents in English for specifically Scandinavian educational concepts. This demonstrated very clearly the disadvantages involved in asking students to provide their own information, unless they are given more preliminary help than we provided.

A transformation task based on a short piece from the *Sun* was much more successful, and enabled the students to regain their confidence in their writing abilities. The text contained every tabloid feature imaginable, including totally irrelevant information, salacious puns and highly suggestive and negative vocabulary. The task was to rewrite the piece for a serious newspaper, in an appropriate style, and including only the relevant information. The *Sun* text was analysed in class prior to the writing exercise, and the results were generally speaking acceptable. The students had begun to grasp the differences between a neutral and an informal style, and between relevant and irrelevant information.

We then decided to move on to informative text types with a persuasive tone, and accordingly looked at extracts from two British University brochures, in which the surroundings of the two universities were described, i.e. the towns themselves and the amenities they offered. The one extract was highly evaluative, with a considerable number of positive value judgements; the other was, by comparison, sober. The texts were structured in similar ways, and the type of information included was also similar. The students were asked to compare the two texts for homework, and their findings were discussed and systematised in class. The writing task comprised writing a similar extract describing the town of Aarhus; they could choose between a sober and a more fulsome style, and were to include the kind of information that they thought would be of interest to foreign university students. Very few of them chose, in fact, to use highly positive vocabulary, as they had found the more sober British brochure more convincing. This task, then, required them to make deliberate stylistic choices as well as choices concerning type of information.

3.4. More radical transformations

The above examples illustrate some of the ways in which we have presented text types and got the students to write similar, or more sober, texts. At the examination, however, they are usually expected to produce text types that differ from the source material. One of the first tasks we gave them where they were expected to do a complete transformation involved the writing of a leaflet. They were given a series of articles from *The Times* dealing with the uproar that arose in Britain when Mrs Edwina Currie claimed that the majority of British eggs were contaminated with salmonella. These articles contained a great deal of information about government measures taken to encourage the production of healthy eggs, about the precautions that consumers were recommended to take to ensure that they were not affected by possibly contaminated eggs, and about the groups of people, such as old people and pregnant women, who were particularly vulnerable. Some of the advice of the various experts quoted in the newspaper was to some extent contradictory; some experts minimised the risk, others might have exaggerated it. The task was to produce a leaflet, issued by the Ministry of Health, the purpose of which was to reassure the public and to suggest the kind of precautions that it would be advisable to take. Any information or arguments used were to be taken from the series of articles. The students were not given a model, as we had no model leaflet to show them. Instead, we discussed such features as format, layout (including highlighting of particular points), type of information, inclusion of expert opinion, use of direct address, style, and tone, with the majority of the suggestions being put forward by the students themselves. As it happened, the Ministry of Health did subsequently produce a kind of leaflet, in the form of a full-page advertisement which appeared in the daily press. Having produced their own leaflets, to which they had given considerable thought, the students were quickly able to analyse the authentic version and see where it resembled or differed from their own. This was an approach that was felt to be satisfactory by all of us. In the event, the students were critical of the genuine text, and not without reason, as it tended to blur the issue. One advantage of analysing an authentic text after they have produced their own is the subsequent realisation on the part of the students that the perfect model does not necessarily exist, and that in any case the way in which a given text is approached is certainly open to discussion. Students tend very often to want cast-iron solutions, and the discovery that these very seldom exist, and that there is no definitive text, no perfect model, is an important part of the process of learning to write. Choices always have to be made, and different people will probably make different choices, depending to some extent on the circumstances.

3.5. Translation as transformation

The types of text transformation I have described so far have all involved transforming an English text into another English text. We also transform Danish texts into English ones, and English texts into Danish ones. In some instances, a more or less straightforward translation is required, as the new target group and the purpose of the new text are defined as being the same as the original ones. For example, one examination paper included a translation of part of the opening paragraph of Gimson's *An Introduction to the Pronunciation of English*, the instructions being that the text was to form the opening paragraph of a Danish version for Danes studying English phonetics.

In other instances, however, the students are told that the text is to be transformed/translated, because the purpose of the new text is different and/or the target group is different. The first question in the 1991 examination paper is such an instance. The Danish text was written for a Danish audience, and included such statements as: 'In England they have the B.A. system, which has been widely discussed in Denmark over the past few years' and 'In England, lectures only last for 50 minutes' (my translation of the Danish). It would not make much sense to the English audience for whom the new text was intended if these statements were translated directly. It was therefore necessary to add some information about the Danish university system; at the time that the text was written, the B.A. did not exist in Denmark, the first degree requiring a minimum of four years' study. This would need to be explained to the English audience, and, of course, the pronoun 'they' should have been changed to 'you'. Similarly, the English university readers did not need to be told the length of their lectures; what they did need to know was that in Denmark lectures (or classes) typically extend over two 45-minute periods. The Danish text also contained some negative remarks about English methods of teaching, which needed to be toned down in order to be acceptable to the new readership. In this type of transformation/translation exercise, the students are altogether given a free hand. They may, for instance, restructure the text if they see fit, they may omit certain points or add others, they may change dialogue into reported speech, and so on; on the other hand, they may decide to keep fairly close to the original text, restricting themselves to the kind of changes suggested above, which would make the text suitable for its new purpose and new audience. What we do require, however, is that they should make comments on any changes that they make and that they should justify them. Conversely, if they make no changes at all, when it has been suggested that some might be necessary, they should be able to explain why none have been made.

3.6. Students' comments on choices

The comments that the students are required to make at the examination are a valuable component, and particularly useful in the work they do throughout the course. They are, however, not always popular, and it takes some initial persuasion to make the students accept the fact that they will derive benefit from them – which most of them do come to acknowledge. The usual complaint is that they take time, and a few students claim that by the time they have completed the task, they have forgotten what decisions they made, if indeed, they consciously made any. It is in particular the latter group that most definitely need to develop the habit of formulating comments, since it is virtually impossible to produce an effective text without making conscious choices.

The first thing that students have to realise is that choices are always available to them. It is, perhaps, most obvious with regard to the information that they choose to include and that which they elect to omit. In some tasks it is, admittedly, self-evident that certain points are relevant, and others are not. But even what seems self-evident to one person does not necessarily seem so to another, and comments on why points have been included or excluded can be useful to the teacher, as they may make him or her regard the text in a new, and sometimes more favourable, light. The structure of a text very often also warrants a comment. The student may have had a particular reason for a structure which does not immediately strike the teacher as being the most obvious one. This is particularly the case if one has already marked several papers which have adopted similar structures, and suddenly encounters one which is totally different. Style and vocabulary are clear instances where conscious choices have to be made. Admittedly, the students do not at this stage master a wide range of styles from a productive point of view, even though in the course of the first two years they become increasingly better at analysing different styles. Most of them can, however, cope with a relatively informal style and a rather more formal one, and in all the tasks they perform they have to decide which is the more appropriate. This also involves deciding whether the sentence structure they use should be relatively simple (as, for instance, in a tourist brochure they were asked to produce for foreigners with a limited knowledge of English) or reasonably complex, and whether the vocabulary should be on the colloquial or the more formal side. Sometimes, as for instance in a humorous text, which they have on occasion had the opportunity to write if they chose to adopt a humorous approach, a mixture of colloquialisms and formal vocabulary can be appropriate. Another choice that frequently has to be made is whether or not to employ direct address. This was a relevant choice to make in question 2 in the 1991 examination paper, and the most successful answers did in fact use direct address, combined with a conversational, and sometimes humorous, style. Some of these candidates also appropriately justified their choice on the grounds that they were writing to entertain, as well as inform, their readers, and that this column was a weekly feature in which the writer wanted to give an impression of intimacy with the reader.

I think it would be fair to say that the comments that the students make in the course of their day-to-day work have two functions. The first, and the main one, is to make them consider, consciously, how to deal with a text and how to produce the desired effect on the reader. The comments are thus part of the process of learning to write effectively. The other function is to enter into a dialogue with the teacher. Once we know that they have made a particular choice deliberately, and why they did so, we are better able to help them see that it was not necessarily the best choice to make. Also, the kind of comments that many of the students make often focus on the doubts they have had: they can be uncertain about a particular lexical item or point of grammar; they may realise when they have completed a task that the text is not sufficiently cohesive, but cannot see how to improve it; they may have aimed at a formal style and have failed to achieve it, but are not quite certain what has gone wrong. Such comments make it much easier to help the student improve his or her work, because they show awareness of a problem; without the comments, the teacher could not possibly know that this awareness existed. Finally, a number of students comment on the task itself, pointing out where the difficulties lay, or why they felt that it was an unsatisfactory or implausible task. These are not the kind of comments that we recommend them to make at the examination – although if they really do discover some real deficiency in a question, we tell them they should certainly draw attention to it, tactfully – but they do provide us with very helpful feedback on the acceptability of the work we give them to do.

4. Feedback

The students' comments can function, then, as a kind of feedback for the teacher. But we also have to give them feedback on their work, and it is here that my main reservations about this type of teaching come in. Each student's work is individual, and different from everyone else's, so individual feedback has to be given if each student is to make progress. This usually takes the form of a typewritten commentary, in which we begin by specifying the good features of the text, so the student knows what is acceptable, and why it is. We then point out the general shortcomings, such as inappropriate style, lack of coherence, irrelevant information, and finally give numbered comments on particular points, including actual mistakes of language. In some cases, we even rewrite passages in order to demonstrate how the style or coherence could be improved. This kind of feedback is obviously time-consuming; the question, too, is how efficient and effective it really is. The students are greatly appreciative, and claim that they learn a great deal from these detailed comments, but this does not always prevent them from making the same mistakes (textual and linguistic) again. It is in particular the recurrence of surface errors that is irritating. I have, however, recently adopted the procedure of merely underlining recurrent or elementary mistakes, and have told the students concerned to correct them and then show them to me. This is actually effective, as most students can correct such mistakes, or see that their suggestion is wrong, so this could be a viable method of eradicating at least persistent surface errors. (In parenthesis, I could mention the student who discovered, to her embarrassment, that fourteen of her underlined mistakes were missing apostrophes. Her comment was that she would not have been aware of this if I had simply corrected them.) Fortunately, too, as the course progresses, and students become used to our typical comments, we can resort in some instances to briefer remarks, referring them to earlier pieces of work, or we can adopt a more elliptic style. But basically, the problem of time is still a major one and seems to be insoluble.

5. Student reaction

It remains to give some indication of student reactions to the new course in writing skills. No such course is the favourite discipline of the majority of university students, and ours are no exception. They can see the value of the teaching and the practice, but when it comes down to it, most of them would say that the study of literature is the most enthralling part of the degree course. Having said that, I would stress that the overwhelming reaction to our present method of teaching is positive. Students generally enjoy the challenge of the different types of task, and even though a few rather lost souls complain that they 'always seem to get it wrong', they, too, experience a sense of achievement and a feeling of enlightenment when they finally begin to get it right. There is the occasional mumbled protest that we are trying to turn them into journalists, which is due to a misconception of the objectives of the course but which renewed explanation can turn into a (sometimes grudging) acknowledgement of the inherent value of analysing and producing a variety of text types. There is also the occasional complaint that there is no scope for true creativity in the tasks they are asked to perform, although the people who voice such complaints readily admit that a return to the What-I-did-in-my-summer-holidays type of essay would be a retrograde step. To give them an opportunity to express themselves freely, we did, however, this year set the second-year students a piece of writing entitled 'The Journey' or 'Journeys'. We discussed at some length the different ways in which the topic could be approached and the different genres that could be used, and the results were surprisingly good, ranging from poems to short stories and philosophical reflections. The effects of the practice the students had had in writing a variety of text types were, gratifyingly, apparent; it was evident that the majority of the students had become accustomed to considering the effect that a particular style, structure and form of text would have on the reader, and in a great number of instances what they wrote did indeed have the effect they had aimed at.

It is towards the middle of the second year that the students not only begin to reap the benefits of the hard work they have put into the course, in the form of a greatly increased understanding of language and textuality, but also become aware of the frequently considerable progress they have made. The consequent sense of accomplishment and satisfaction takes some of them by surprise. Not infrequently a student will say: 'I am only just beginning to realise how much I have learned.' This, understandably, increases motivation and promotes, in general, positive attitudes towards the course. Another motivating factor is indubitably the word processor, to which an increasing number of students are gaining access. Since certain text types owe at least part of their effectiveness to their layout, students experiment with the word processor and often produce extremely professional-looking pieces of work. This tends to have a spin-off effect on the text itself, as the students' level of ambition rises with regard to all aspects of their work.

In conclusion, I would like to add a qualification. It could be assumed from my largely enthusiastic account that the approach to teaching writing skills outlined in this article always leads to improved language proficiency. This is not necessarily the case. A very small number of students have confirmed my original fears by acquiring a superficial acquaintance with the tricks of the trade of text production, while remaining relatively impervious to the demands of accuracy. This, in all fairness, also applied to a small number of students taught in accordance with the grammar-translation method or the translation-summary-essay approach. It is difficult to determine how such students can best be helped. By and large, however, the students taught by this method make perceptible progress, mainly, I think, because they respond to the challenge of demanding, interesting and generally speaking realistic tasks. We can, on the whole, claim to have 'satisfied customers', which is probably the best recommendation there is.

Appendix: Tim's silly letters

The following two letters have both been written in a totally inappropriate style. The first is a letter from a bookshop to a customer telling him that a book has arrived; the second is a holiday postcard sent to a friend.

Your task is to rewrite the letter and the postcard in an appropriate format and style. You will probably find that you have to make some major changes; for example, it may not be appropriate to include all the information given in the original in your rewritten version.

1. LETTER FROM BOOKSHOP

Wednesday

Dear Joe,

Do you remember me? We had quite a long chat about six weeks ago when you dropped into our bookshop to order some stuff. Actually, you were a bit upset at the time about how little we'd actually got in stock and so on. I hope the manager was able to explain everything to you alright!

Anyway, one of the books you ordered has come at last! It's that one by Anne Raimes, called 'Techniques in Teaching Writing' or something like that. Actually, I'm afraid the price has gone up a bit. We told you it would cost £5.30, but there's been a new price list come out, and they've put it up to £7.75. Shocking, isn't it? Well, I suppose that's inflation for you.

So, any time you like to come in, the book will be here waiting for you. Well, I say 'any time', but actually you're supposed to come and get it during the next two weeks, otherwise we have to send it back again, which would be a bit of a shame really, considering.

It'll be wonderful to see you again when you come for the book!

All best wishes,

Sandra

2. HOLIDAY POSTCARD

Apollo Hotel Apartments
Grivas Dighenis Ave.
Larnaca
CYPRUS

Wednesday, May 11th, 1990

Mrs Jenny Hargreaves
3, Birch Avenue
Salisbury
Wilts   SB4 3RW

Dear Mrs Hargreaves,

This is to inform you that my husband, James, and I
have arrived without incident at our destination,
Larnaca in Cyprus. The average daily temperature at
present is 28° Celsius, and the average sea temperature is 18°. We therefore spend a considerable amount
of time each day at the beach, where we swim and lie
in the sun.

We judge the food served in restaurants here to be of
a high standard, especially with respect to flavour,
and also to be relatively inexpensive. Consequently,
we dine out frequently, despite the fact that our
apartment has cooking facilities. I regret that James
usually becomes slightly inebriated at meals, being
unable to resist indulgence in the low-priced local
wines and spirits.

Yours sincerely,

Freda G Finchley (Mrs)

The Role of Stylistics in EFL

Judith E. Munat

1. Defining ESP

Today much language teaching centers on E.S.P. (English for Specialized Purposes), or in layman's terms, English as an instrument of communication in a specialized field of study or work. Thus, one can learn English as a 'tool' to decipher medical texts, or as a means of communication in the field of tourism, or as the language of international finance. This presumes, naturally, the existence of a common language core that must be mastered before embarking upon a more specialized or limited area of the syllabus, but it is to one of these specialized areas that most students of English will be devoting a good part of their language study.

Some doubt is legitimate, of course, as to whether mastery of a language can be viewed merely as the key to Pandora's box in a limited field of study. But even without resolving that Hamletic doubt, two practical advantages to such an approach are immediately evident: first, the student will presumably be more highly motivated in his language acquisition if he has a goal which is directly related to his field of primary professional or academic interest; second, the teaching objectives will consequently be circumscribed, allowing the definition of a more manageable syllabus (usually theme or topic based). Ideally, in such a situation, both student and teacher will get rapid and positive feedback as the units on the syllabus are mastered.

In practical terms, then, the language syllabus for students in medicine or economics or law, for example, will first address the task of teaching or revising the common core, after which the focus will be on the language of the specialized field. The teacher will rely on one (or more) of the area-specific textbooks available on the market, adapting the material, if necessary, to suit the students' needs but confining herself to area-specific content, i.e., the topics, language functions, structures and lexis which most frequently occur in the specific area of interest.

However, outside the field of ESP, as Davies states (1985:18), 'one sometimes has the impression that students are being taught "English for no particular purpose at all"'. What happens, for example, in the case of university degree courses in English language and literature? What is the 'specialized' language of literature? If, as has been suggested above, in other fields it is theoretically possible to identify the language functions, structures and lexis occurring most frequently, and limit the syllabus to the teaching of this area-specific language, is it possible to define a range of distinct purposes for EFL students of literature, selecting and delimiting the appropriate language forms?

2. The ESP of Literary Studies

In theory, the student of literature should be intent on absorbing the entire corpus (i.e., the entire English language) since *all* language can be used as a means of literary expression. This vast category, in fact, embraces all possible linguistic communicative functions, in that literature may at one time or another call upon any variety (even technical registers can be adopted for purposes of irony).

Therefore, how can we, as teachers of language in a literature program, define a language syllabus which is both relevant and yet manageable? Once the basic language foundations have been laid, what language will be most relevant to the student of literature as he progresses in his studies? The perspective from which we approach this question will determine the choices made by the English language teacher in the humanistic faculties and, more precisely, in degree courses in English literature.

While the solution proffered is often that of English for Academic Purposes (EAP), this does not, in reality, respond to our needs. EAP merely specifies a series of language skills required at university level such as those of producing an academic essay, note-taking, translation or reading skills, but gives little or no indication as to language content. We must, instead, seek to define an area of language study which will be applicable to the literary studies of our students and subsequently establish the content of an appropriate course syllabus.

The assumption on which our proposed syllabus is based is that the study of literature requires on the part of the student the *recognition* of as wide a *variety of registers* as possible, and even beyond this, the ability to *identify* the distinguishing *linguistic features* of each of these varieties or registers along with a *knowledge* of the *social and pragmatic factors* determining such language choices. Ideally, this will culminate in the development of a literary sensitivity which will allow the student to make the necessary link between authorial choice and effect on the reader. And the students will also learn to manipulate an appropriate range of registers in their own use of the language.

Therefore, the study of a range of discourse types, entailing the stylistic (lexical, grammatical and phonological features) as well as pragmatic analysis[1] of texts[2] and the acquisition of the metalanguage serving for their description is, we propose, what constitutes the ESP of literary studies. This should also include the acquisition of a discourse grammar,[3] (i.e., the understanding of the functioning of cohesion and coherence in discourse, the macro-structure of individual texts, and their interactional nature).

It is important, before going on to a more practical discussion of these principles, to make a distinction between *literary stylistics* as that based on models of practical criticism and *linguistic stylistics* directed at linguistic analysis of both literary and non-literary texts. We adopt the term in the latter sense, as a 'bridge discipline between linguistics and literature,' in Carter's words (1988:161) or, stated more simply, as a means to the comprehension and interpretation of all texts, literary and non-literary, spoken and written, seen in relation to their communicative function.

3. Practical Discourse Stylistics in the EFL classroom

But how can this be accomplished in actual practice? Let us translate into more concrete and practical terms such a theoretical justification for stylistics in the EFL classroom by attempting to explain its application in the confines of a syllabus for university students of English language and literature, with the following pedagogical principles and objectives in mind:

1) the teacher's role is that of facilitator, providing as input the necessary metalanguage and models of analysis, but encouraging students to make their own discovery of language variations as a problem-solving activity;

2) integrated language skills are practiced in a communicatively authentic manner within a workshop/seminar structure[4] in which both receptive and productive capacities are developed;

3) the students' language sensitivity is developed, resulting in increased critical and analytical capacities as well as the ability to produce an appropriate range of registers.

These are the guiding principles behind the syllabus which is proposed in Figure 1, which entails gradual familiarization with a variety of registers through the examination of authentic spoken and written texts. By developing a recognition of the subtleties of stylistic variation both in relation to the author's purpose and to other pragmatic and social factors such as function, medium, relationship between text and audience, between text and context, etc., the student will learn to respond to a text in terms of its communicative function and not as a fixed, immutable object. In the process she will become a more effective listener and reader and, hopefully, speaker and writer as well.

I. Introductory unit
A. Examination of 6 or 7 (oral and written) brief extracts of different varieties
B. Class discussion of distinguishing features
C. Synthesis and reordering of 'stylistic' descriptive features
D. Teacher input: appropriate labels (metalanguage)
E. Considerations of influence of (oral vs. written) medium

II. Study of telegraphic (written) varieties
A. Focus on headlines/book titles/telegrams/graffiti
B. Working groups: identification of stylistic differences
C. Teacher-assisted reflections on features determined by differences in writer's purpose/spatial restrictions
D. Task: write your own telegram/headline for a news article

III. Study of formulaic (written and oral) language
A. Focus on greeting cards/popular songs/advertising jingles/nursery rhymes
B. Working groups to identify distinctive linguistic features and determining factors
C. Teacher input: similarities with literary genres

IV. Focus on advertising media
A. TV commercials (view and discuss)/press advertising (group analysis)
B. Contrastive stylistic features
C. Reflections on how target audience and product advertised determine language content and form
D. Teacher input: similarities between poetry/advertising
E. Task: write your own advertisement

V. Study of degrees of 'orality'
A. Focus on conversation/interviews/lectures/public speech/news broadcasts
B. Listening exercises with tapes, videos
C. Teacher input: terms of relevant phonological analysis
D. Working groups: analysis of characteristic features
E. Teacher-assisted reflection on oral extemporaneous speech vs. texts written to be read
F. Tasks: reproduction of oral models in class
    1) levels of formality (e.g. conversation between friends/family/strangers)
    2) social functions (e.g. interviews professor/student, writer/journalist)
    3) language functions and participation (group debate on a topic of current interest/give a persuasive speech)
G. Reflections on interplay between social relationships/language functions/ planned-unplanned speech
H. Input: metalanguage and models of conversational analysis

VI. Focus on newspaper language
A. Class study of 6/7 newspapers
B. Group work: identification of 1) different varieties in one newspaper 2) different target audiences of each newspaper 3) different content and style of single articles
C. Close-up study of formal structure of news article
D. Contrast in medium ('oral' TV news/written news article)
E. Contrast in functions (expressing opinions in editorial comment/narrative description of event in sports commentary)
F. Task: write your own news article

VII. Similarities between literary and non-literary varieties
A. Comparison between sports commentary/news articles/narrative description of event
B. Comparison of adverts/songs/nursery rhymes/poetry
C. Comparison of conversation/speech presentation in novel/dramatic dialogue
D. Comparison between lectures/public speech/dramatic monologue

4. Discussion of Syllabus

The syllabus proposed is the result of five years of didactic experimentation in the Faculty of Letters at the University of Pisa with students in a four-year degree program in English language and literature. It introduces, in the second year of their language studies, the concept of language variation in relation to social and pragmatic factors, in a Varieties of English course, the only course in the language curriculum which is *not* orientated toward the acquisition of a specific skill (listening and speaking, reading, writing, translation, etc.) or knowledge-based (phonetics, grammar). It is, instead, an integrated-skills course, directed at sensitizing the students to language in use, and can be expanded or reduced to contain as much, or as little, material as classroom hours permit.

By the second year of their university studies, our students are presumed to have attained a level of language proficiency approximately equivalent to that of Cambridge First Certificate (intermediate). In their first year they have revised grammar, studied English phonetics, done a reading skills course familiarizing them with different text types, and a writing course in which they have learned to express requests, complaints and personal opinions, as well as produce chronological narratives, descriptions, etc.

Our proposed syllabus may be confined to an academic year but should ideally continue at the third and fourth years of the degree program to focus more specifically on literary genres, studying the language of the works read in the literature courses. The approach to literature should be identical to that used in dealing with non-literary texts, based on the conviction that a 'special language of literature' does not exist, but is instead simply a question of a greater density of certain features in comparison to non-literary texts (see Carter, 1987).

Our practical 'discourse stylistics' begins with the presentation of a variety of (unidentified) one- or two-line extracts from longer (spoken and written) texts, literary and non-literary:[5] headlines, poetry, conversation, advertising, news reports, technical register, narrative, etc.. With the extracts in front of them, the students are asked to 'guess' the text types or varieties and then to try and explain the reason for their guesses in terms of language features. This initial exercise helps the students to transform their frequently correct intuitions about language use into a concrete description of linguistic features as justification for such intuitions. In addition it will encourage them to think in terms of WHY given language choices are made (considering purpose, as well as contingent contextual factors such as time or space available, relationship between writer or speaker and audience, type and number of audience participants, etc.). The students are guided towards reflection on the factors which shape each text by means of pertinent questions.

Figure 1 (opposite page): Oral exam question types

Following this introductory exercise the students are presented with, or asked to seek their own samples of, a wide range of text types: from Christmas cards to book titles, from TV commercials to press advertising, from extemporaneous conversation to interviews and debates, from newspaper varieties (headlines, news reports, sports commentary, editorial comment, reviews, etc.) to TV and radio news broadcasts, from public speech to dramatic monologue and conversation in the novel (leading to the analysis of literary genre at the more advanced stages).

The order of presentation of this abundant material is determined by a contrastive approach: either a contrast in medium (e.g., oral political speech *versus* written editorial comment, oral TV commercials *versus* written press advertising, spoken news broadcasts *versus* printed newspaper articles, etc.) or contrasting purposes within the same medium (e.g., headlines/book titles, university lecture/political speech, etc.).

The didactic exploitation of each text varies according to the type (e.g., from the phonological study of accents and dialects in conversations, to creative writing assignments such as that of producing an original press advertisement, to listening comprehension activities connected with TV commercials and recorded conversations). Much of the work in class is directed at recognition of the distinguishing features of the variety being examined and the identification of the factors that determined these features. A workshop classroom structure with groups of students working together to discuss a given text and later reporting their findings to the entire class provides a student-centered classroom as well as authentic speaking practice.

Our syllabus is a freely-branching one rather than rigidly defined. The reason for this choice is the diversity of each group of students. The collective class personality will change each term – some student groups will be less proficient linguistically and more timid and less dynamic in group interaction, while others will prove to be in excellent command of the spoken language, volatile, and ready to strike out in unforseen directions. These differences must be allowed for by a flexible syllabus.

The order of presentation of the discourse types to be studied is not necessarily fixed, but can be determined in the course of the term. The only guidelines are those of 1) moving from linguistically simpler texts (such as book titles or greeting cards), to texts of greater linguistic density (such as printed advertising, TV commercials, extemporaneous conversation), and 2) juxtaposing texts in terms of their similarities and/or contrastive features.

4.1. Advertising variety

By way of illustration, let us outline the contents of a teaching unit dealing with press advertising, which, given its use of both visual (colors, illustrations, graphic layout, type size, etc.) and linguistic means, offers a particularly rich context in relation to which the communicative value of the message can be examined. Advertising variety may be presented following the study of TV commercials for contrastive analysis of oral and written mediums having the same purpose, and possibly followed by the study of a simple poem for a comparison of stylistic features present in both text types.

After working groups have analyzed three or four advertisements, they can present a synthesis of their findings to the class, and a composite list of distinguishing features may be compiled on the blackboard and logically re-ordered to something like the following, which will then constitute a descriptive model for written advertising variety that can serve as a basis of comparison for other varieties (e.g. poetry):

Prosodic features
  use of punctuation to mimic speech effects
  alliteration, rhyme, assonance, etc.

Informality features typical of oral discourse
  contracted forms
  use of direct address (*you, we* personal pronouns)
  colloquialisms/slang

Syntactic/lexical features
  minor sentences/ellipsis
  structural parallelism
  extensive use of adjectives (comparatives/superlatives)
  lexical sets (often with double meanings[6])

Stylistic devices at the semantic level
  clichés/puns/plays on words
  proverbs
  literary references/quotations
  figures of speech such as metaphor/simile

This close-up examination of the language of advertising will serve as a reinforcement of our earlier claim that 'literary language' does not, in fact, constitute a distinct language variety, but shares many features with other non-literary varieties.

But class discussion of advertisements will lead beyond a purely linguistic analysis to the many subtleties of implicit persuasion which can be related to the intended purpose, to the topic (i.e., product advertised) and to the audience to which the advertisement is directed: contrastive analysis of advertisements for similar products directed at different audiences (e.g. a car advertisement intended for men or women) will give further impetus to the discussion.

4.2. Conversation

Another area of particular interest which might be presented as a contrast to the 'orality' of TV commercials, is the study of extemporaneous conversation (either on cassettes or video tapes), which will include purely phonological aspects (accent, dialects) as well as consideration of supra-segmental features such as tone-units, pitch, stress, speed, loudness, pauses etc. and their role in communicating the message. Also the study of extra-linguistic features such as gesticulation, facial expression, body position, etc. (when videotapes of conversations are available) will reveal information about the speakers and their relationships.

Levels of formality in speech are also an important aspect of conversational study for the EFL student who is still learning appropriate code-switching, and focus on non-fluency features and lack of planning occurring in authentic conversation (e.g., grammatical 'errors', hesitations, slips of the tongue, overlapping, randomness of subject matter, etc.) offers an interesting contrast to the 'idealized' dialogues presented in language coursebooks. Also, the dependence of the message on surrounding physical context (e.g., '*This* is what I mean.' 'Over *there*.' 'Look!' (at *what*?) 'Pick *it* up.') is useful food for thought, as are reflections on the necessity of using hesitations, fillers and other non-fluency features in highly informal conversation to avoid conveying an impression of 'affectedness'.

While detailed conversational analysis is beyond our scope, some discussion of turn-taking, adjacency pairs and the pragmatics of holding the floor could be usefully carried out, in order to lead to wider considerations of textuality: how are single turns marked, and how do these fit together to create the boundaries of the macro text that we define as 'conversation'?.

This study of conversational phenomena will later serve as a basis for contrastive analysis with speech in the novel and with dramatic dialogue.

4.3. Newspapers

Our final practical illustration deals with the study of newspapers, which might precede or follow the study of TV and radio news broadcasting, as a contrast between texts sharing identical purposes but different mediums: one written to be read and the other written to be spoken.

The students should be given several different newspapers, from tabloid to quality press, and allowed to leaf through them to satisfy their curiosity. Only then they should be asked how many different varieties they have found (e.g. letters, advertisements, reviews, editorial comment, sports commentary, comic strips, etc.), which of these constitute sub-varieties of 'journalese' and which, instead, can be identified as a distinct variety. Finally, what are the features which distinguish the varieties identified?

The study of headline variety could easily be the object of a separate teaching unit, suggesting a contrast with other written varieties of a telegraphic nature such as book titles or telegrams or personal notes. What are the syntactic differences and the reasons determining such differences?

The next suggested focus of study is that of the differences between individual newspapers, both in terms of their intended audience and their political positions. Several working groups might be given a list of questions such as the following on which to reflect:

(1) Who do you think would read this newspaper? Explain the reasons for your reply.

(2) Is the *type* of news reported different in the various newspapers or does the difference lie in the *way* the news is reported? Why?

(3) How do graphic features (photos, type size, etc.) contribute to the message? How do they vary from one newspaper to another? Why?

A more detailed study of the content and style of single articles can be carried out by providing three or four articles on the same topic or news event, drawn from different newspapers. A comparative analysis should include graphic features, headlines, story focus (as determined by type and ordering of information) as well as language form (lexis and syntax), attempting in each case to identify the factors which determine these differences.

This description of the detailed content and aims of three units on our syllabus will, we hope, serve as an illustration of our approach to language study, focusing on the relationship between form and the factors determining that form such as medium, audience, speaker or writer goal, relationships between participants, etc. This view of language as a flexible communicative process rather than concentration on the text as a static object should: 1) create a greater capacity in the student to manipulate language; 2) develop a sensitivity in recognizing how language is exploited in order to attain a given effect; and 3) provide the necessary metalanguage to express new concepts about language which will be relevant to the students' literary studies.

5. The Language of Literature

This explanation of our approach to discourse stylistics in the EFL classroom brings us to consider the relevance of literary stylistics in language studies. By having provided students with what Breen and Short (1988) refer to as the 'relevant skills and knowledge' with which to analyze texts from a linguistic perspective, we will enable them to understand how language functions in all contexts, literary and non-literary.

Gower (1986:27) objects that linguistic analysis of a literary text by an EFL learner interferes with the reading of the text because 'the more you focus on language form, the less the students understand what is going on'. We disagree that this is the inevitable result of a language-based approach to the study of literature. On the contrary, we believe that it can provide an added dimension to the reading of a text, aiding the student in the discovery of deeper-level meanings and therefore of reading enjoyment. But stylistics must not be adopted simply to carry out a sterile dissection of the text. Our route is that of a series of consciousness-raising activities leading to an appreciation of the effects of linguistic expression and the subtleties of language variation.

Assuming a fundamental interest in both *language* and *literature* on the part of our students, the study of language as the stuff of which literature is made cannot but be relevant. Literary texts in the language classroom must simply be seen as further 'genuine samples of a wide range of styles, registers and text-types' (Duff and Maley, 1990) by indicating the similarities with many of the non-literary varieties studied earlier. In fact, as Short and Candlin (1986:91) state, it is difficult to make a purely linguistic distinction between literature and other kinds of language in that there are no particular features or set of features found in literature that do not reappear in other kinds of texts.

Therefore, our study of language in literary texts is directed at pointing out similarities with text types studied previously, concentrating initially on those literary texts which most lend themselves to a comparative analysis with non-literary varieties. Our problem-solving approach encourages the students first to read and express their intuitive response to a text, identifying the salient or foregrounded[7] linguistic features only afterward and only if they are felt to be relevant in relation to textual function. The range of language discovery activities that can be adopted in studying literary passages is vast and can be gleaned from the many valid textbooks available on the market dedicated to teaching literature in the language classroom. It is beyond the scope of this article to suggest specific classroom activities; we wish only to indicate methodological principles. Let us repeat yet once again that stylistic analysis must be subservient to the reading of a text and not an end unto itself.

Finally, we wish to confute Cook's (1986) objection that the study of brief extracts taken from longer literary works will distort the meaning of the text because, he states, internal cohesive ties are broken when a section of text is examined out of its original context. We believe, instead, that if extracts are drawn from longer works which the students have read in their literature courses, familiarity with the entire text will allow them to reconstruct any missing cohesive ties by referring back to the larger context when necessary.

6. Conclusions

In synthesis, we have attempted to demonstrate the application of an approach to the teaching of language as the substance of literary discourse, suggesting that all that is part of a language-based approach to literature constitutes the 'specialized purpose' language for EFL students of literature. Thus an ESP syllabus embracing the forms and functions of language studied in a wide variety of text-types and registers, including, but not limited to, literary genres, is our answer to ESP for literary studies. The mastery of a range of registers or varieties, each with its distinctive forms and appropriate social functions, is essential to the learner of a foreign language (Adamson, 1989:235) and even more so, to the understanding and appreciation of the multi-faceted variety of literature.

The appropriate metalanguage, only a small part of the syllabus, is taught in function of the expression of relevant concepts. Far more important are the concepts themselves, related to language variation in a social and pragmatic framework. Encouraging sensitivity to the range of styles, registers and text types offered by literary texts, stimulating curiosity about the way language is manipulated, and developing the capacity to understand the relationship between language choice and the factors determining such choices are the ultimate goals of our ESP syllabus for students of literature.

Notes

1. Vimala Herman (1983:118) suggests, in fact, that attention to the sociolinguistic and pragmatic aspects of language may be more fruitful than 'undue concentration on syntax and phonology'.
2. We use 'text' to mean 'any well-formed and interpretable linguistic utterance within a communicative context', which means that a text may be only one word or many words, according to Van Peer's (1988:269) definition.
3. The term 'discourse' as used here comprises all aspects of communication, whether spoken or written, including the message or text, the addresser and addressee and their immediate context (Wales, 1989:129).
4. Seminar format maximizes involvement of students while the teacher's role is less dominant and the students are therefore more inclined to share their views and ideas, according to Verdonk (1988:243).
5. This idea comes from experimentation carried out in the design of a stylistics course for native speakers at the University of Lancaster (Breen and Short, 1988).
6. Such as 'in a class of its own' where *class* is part of a lexical set relating to school.
7. *Foregrounding* is here intended to mean any language pattern or any linguistic deviation from a background of neutral or unmarked language which has communicative relevance (i.e., is presumably a conscious authorial choice aiming at a specific effect) in the context in which it appears.

References

Adamson, S. 1988. 'With double tongue: diglossia, stylistics and the teaching of English', in Short (1988).

Brumfit, C. and Carter, R. (eds.). 1986. *Literature and Language Teaching*. Oxford: O.U.P.

Breen, M.P. and Short, M. 1988. 'Alternative Approaches to Teaching Stylistics to Beginners', in *Parlance*, Journal of Poetics and Linguistics Association, 1/2.

Carter, R. 1987. *Vocabulary: Applied Linguistic Perspectives*. London: Allen & Unwin.

Carter, R. 1988. 'What is stylistics and why can we teach it in different ways?', in Short (1988).

Cook, G. 1986. 'Texts, extracts and stylistic texture', in Brumfit and Carter (1986).

Davies, E.E. 1985. 'Looking at style with advanced EFL learners', *ELT Journal* 39/1.

Duff, A. and Maley A. 1990. *Literature*. Oxford: O.U.P.

Gower, Roger. 1986. 'Can stylistic analysis help the EFL learner to read literature?', *ELT Journal* 40/2, April 1986.

Herman, V. 1985. 'Introduction: Literariness and linguistics', *Prose Studies* 6/5.

Short, M. (ed.). 1988. *Reading, Analysing and Teaching Literature*. Hong Kong: Longman.

Short, M. and Candlin, C. 1986. 'Teaching study skills for English literature', in Brumfit and Carter (1986).

van Peer, W. 1988. 'How to do things with texts. Towards a pragmatic foundation for the teaching of texts', in Short (1988).

Verdonk, P. 1988. 'The language of poetry: the application of literary stylistic theory in university teaching', in Short (1988).

Wales, K. 1989. *A Dictionary of Stylistics*. Singapore: Longman.

Using Mini-sagas in Language Teaching[1]

Stephen Keeler

The mini-saga is a relatively new literary genre. It has neither the history nor the pedigree of the sonnet, say, or the novel or short story. And therefore it carries little or none of the literary and academic baggage often so intimidating to non-native speakers and foreign language students as they approach 'great works'.

To qualify as a mini-saga a piece of writing must fulfil three conditions. First of all, a mini-saga is *exactly* fifty words long: forty-nine or fifty-one and it's not a mini-saga! Secondly, it may have a title of up to fifteen (additional) words. Thirdly, it should tell a story. To describe a mood or a scene is not enough. Mini-sagas are 'hot-rod versions of the Odyssey ... megalosaurus-sized mouthfuls, designed to tease reader and writer alike'.[2]

A brief history is necessary. Although undoubtedly used by writers and teachers as a perhaps fairly arbitrary device for imposing a creative discipline long before 1982, it was then that the newly named mini-saga made its first 'official' appearance, in a *Telegraph Sunday Magazine*[3] readers' competition in Britain. The judges received 32,000 entries. Similar competitions, now in conjunction with BBC Radio 4, in 1985 and 1986 produced almost 100,000 more. The judges have been prominent British authors, publishers and broadcasters; and although competition entrants have included members of the British royal family, the vast majority of mini-sagas have been written by 'ordinary folk' with an idea. This prize-winning piece was written by an eleven-year-old schoolgirl:

DYING?

Thrown in with a crowd,
the door slams shut.
I hear water.
I feel redness oozing from me
colouring the water.
Gasping for air,
blood runs to my toes.
Knocked out by arms and legs,
I come round

hanging on the washing line –
a red sock
among pale pink laundry.

Lucy Ogbourne[4]

Clearly the mini-saga had been an excellent idea long waiting to be discovered. Its formal appearance released the creative skills of thousands of would-be (and perhaps would-not-be) writers, and it would have been perverse not to publish a collection of the best competition entries. *The Book of Mini-Sagas* (see Note 2) appeared in 1985 and *The Book of Mini-Sagas II* (see Note 4) followed three years later. The two books constitute the only formal source of authentic (i.e. not written for or in connection with language teaching purposes) published mini-sagas, and as such represent the main body of reference for this article. However, it should be noted that of the four hundred or so mini-sagas published in these two books it is this author's belief that fewer than ten per cent will be readily usable in the majority of EFL classrooms. This does not invalidate the case for using mini-sagas in language teaching – thirty-odd short pieces of elegant, clever, accessible writing is a substantial enough body of texts from which to draw. Additionally, the concept itself is easily enough integrated into so-called creative writing tasks.

The most interesting and successful teaching materials are those which are truly educational: materials which generate genuine, personal responses from students by speaking to and inter-relating with them at a personal level and which involve them in activity which has some intrinsic value beyond the walls of the classroom.

It has become axiomatic that not only does a significant part of what we simplify by called the learning process take place subconsciously and incidentally, but that learning cannot be switched on and off at the start and end of lessons. Successful teachers and materials/activity devisers readily accept the obligation to create an acquisition-rich learning environment which will necessarily be unrestrained by institutional brickwork. The arguments for authenticity do not need to be rehearsed on these pages.

Morgan and Rinvolucri[5] point out that 'if unconscious processes are to be enlisted, then the whole person will need to be engaged: we shall no longer be able to rely on the learner's general "motivation" or on the intrinsic charms of the target language to sustain him or her through the years of monotonous drilling and bland role-play'.

Stories seem to have universal appeal. They appear to activate deep-rooted intrinsic tendencies to attempt to make sense of the human condition by communicating our inner narratives to others – perhaps to reassure ourselves that our experiences and reactions are not sinister or eccentric. Whatever the reasons, few people dislike stories and fewer still have no story to tell. This alone makes stories ideal classroom material and Morgan and Rinvolucri (see Note

5) provide a rich source of them, together with creative devices for exploiting them.

This author's claim on behalf of mini-sagas is simply that the published corpus provides an exciting source of text material and that the concept can be exploited in students' writing tasks. Teachers and course/materials devisers often encounter formidable difficulties when researching appropriate authentic and unabridged 'literature' for use at lower and intermediate levels. In an attempt to avoid texts which are too long, which require too intensive treatment or which are culturally over-loaded or cognitively over-sophisticated, we too readily resort to material which is quaint, simplistic, undemanding, linguistically distorted and just plain dull. In methodological terms too there is room for invention and sophistication. It can not only be dull to have to write a short story about 'My Family', it can be a massively intimidating task to have to wrestle with such a literary form even as straightforward as the short story. Mini-sagas offer an alternative approach:

LIFE
AND NUMBERS

Once upon a time
there was
just Me.
I soon realised there were
three of us, then gradually
four. At last there were just
the two of us. All at once four
of us. Suddenly just the two
of us again. Now there is
only Me
as in the beginning.

Frances Politzer[6]

There are at least five good reasons for considering using mini-sagas in language teaching:

1 **Novelty value.** The mini-saga is a relatively new literary form. Students generally respond positively to new types of classroom activities or materials which are enthusiastically presented by the teacher. An initial approach which has worked well is to make enlarged photocopies of between eight and twelve suitable mini-sagas mounted on card and placed around the classroom. When the students enter they are asked to spend ten minutes or so going from card to card reading the mini-sagas. Allow them to make any notes they want and

ask them to choose the text they like best and to be prepared to say a few words about why they like it.

Present the concept of the mini-saga, its rules and a brief history. Students are more likely to respond positively to materials which they know have not been used by generations of students before them.

2 **Length.** So long as they are chosen carefully, mini-sagas are, generally speaking, rather less intimidating than short stories and even poems. There is nothing so unsatisfactory as the literary extract from a longer work.

In another, but related, context Garrison Keillor[7] has written of the self-contained elegance of a fifty-word message and of the conducive discipline it imposes. With the mini-saga you get the complete work and it doesn't take long to read it from cover to cover. It can be read several times without the task becoming tedious and by definition there will always be a limited number of unfamiliar words or expressions. The piece is just so much more accessible. By the same token, the prospect of writing a mini-saga is bound to be less overwhelming than many of the creative writing tasks students are asked to perform, even if inspiration may sometimes not be forthcoming:

WRITING
A MINI-SAGA

Morning.
Blank paper faces
me. This is more difficult
than I thought. Time passes.
Think of a subject. Reject it.
Then another. Pause for a cup
of coffee. Still no inspiration.
Foolish of me to try and
write something like this.
Lunch time. Food for
thought? Just four
more words.

Ian Laing[8]

3 **Flexibility.** Both in terms of subject matter and format this little form allows great scope. Several of the published mini-sagas are in verse and some appear as concrete poems. Writing mini-sagas can allow students to be creative within the range of their language competence. It doesn't have to rhyme. It doesn't have to scan. It doesn't require a large or sophisticated vocabulary and yet it will respond to such treatment.

Perhaps of rather more specific language-teaching interest and value, the process of editing and re-working which is required to produce a piece of exactly fifty words is of immense value. Language has to be manipulated according to the semantic, syntactic and grammatical rules. Such manipulation, engaged in as a secondary process to service the principal task of producing a finished personal text, is not always easy to generate from more conventional methodologies without forfeiting the essentially authentic nature of the task.

4 **Authenticity.** It is easy enough to argue that nothing set by a teacher as part of a course programme can be regarded as truly authentic. This seems to be a particularly unhelpful position to take on authenticity. Students do read (albeit perhaps in their mother tongue) outside the classroom and can therefore be expected to want to read in the foreign language provided they have access to material which is of intrinsic interest and value. Ten or fifteen carefully chosen mini-sagas mounted on reading cards or bound in booklet form *may* excite student interest. Teachers can do no more than offer materials, create the environment and provide the support.

This is often where teachers are tempted to interfere with questions and exercises. Morgan and Rinvolucri warn against what most experienced teachers instinctively know yet so often over-rule, that 'so-called "comprehension" questions at best dilute, at worst destroy'[9] students' enjoyment of a text, whether read or heard. Such questions rarely aid comprehension and are no substitute for authentic dialogue between students (and teacher) on their personal responses to what they have read, heard and even written.

5 **Enjoyment.** Too often left, as I have left it, to the end of such lists as this – or even omitted altogether – enjoyment must be central to our teaching and learning endeavours. The notion that something has to hurt before it can be regarded as being good for you is at least as dubious in education as it is in sport.

Mini-sagas, for the reasons stated above, can be immensely enjoyable. They are often humorous and the best seem to have a twist or a sting in the tail.

Once students begin to write them, many go on to produce them in great numbers. Even relative beginners can produce satisfying work. Mini-saga competitions are often an effective way of getting started, and collections of students' work in magazine form make a satisfying and motivating project. Mini-sagas can be used for reading for pleasure, in recitation programmes, for storytelling, in creative writing work, in radio programme making, to celebrate special occasions, in competitions, as project work, in theme-based programmes, in literary discussions, in linguistic discussions and to develop editing and language manipulation skills. Or maybe you just want to bring a momentary smile of comprehension and appreciation to your students' faces:

A USELESS
BUY

No fun sitting here at the
bottom of the pool writing
letters.
The paper is soggy, and the
envelopes keep getting
stuck.
And my rheumatism is worse.
It will take a day for the
paper to dry out.
I wish I had not bought a
pen that writes under water.

A.C. Foster[10]

Notes

1. Parts of this paper are adapted from an earlier article, 'Using mini-sagas in language teaching', which appeared in *Practical English Teaching* 7/2, December 1986 (London: Mary Glasgow Publications), pp. 23-24.
2. Brian Aldiss, *The Book of Mini-Sagas,* Telegraph Sunday Magazine (Gloucester: Alan Sutton Publishing, 1985), p. 7.
3. *The Telegraph Sunday Magazine* is a features supplement to *The Sunday Telegraph*, a British Sunday newspaper.
4. *The Book of Mini-Sagas II,* Telegraph Sunday Magazine (Gloucester: Alan Sutton Publishing, 1988), p. 41. All four mini-sagas reproduced in this article are © *The Telegraph Sunday Magazine* and are reproduced with the permission of the publisher.
5. John Morgan and Mario Rinvolucri, *Once Upon A Time* (Cambridge: Cambridge University Press, 1983), p. 1.
6. *The Book of Mini-Sagas,* op. cit. p. 38.
7. Garrison Keillor, *We Are Still Married* (London: Faber and Faber, 1990), p. 230.
8. *The Book of Mini-Sagas,* op. cit., p. 244.
9. John Morgan and Mario Rinvolucri, *Once Upon A Time,* op. cit., p. 2.
10. *The Book of Mini-Sagas,* op. cit., p. 42.

Request Strategies in Non-Native and Native Speakers of English

Anna Trosborg

1. Introduction

1.1. Background

With the increasing demand for communicative competence in a second language, the interest in second/foreign language learning and teaching centres more and more on aspects of sociopragmatic competence and discourse competence. However, traditional classroom discourse does not generally promote these skills sufficiently in learners.

Numerous studies have shown that a rigid pattern of classroom interaction and the frequent use of display questions leave learners few opportunities to develop these important aspects of communicative competence (e.g. Trosborg, 1984; Long and Porter, 1985; Loercher, 1986).

In teacher-directed classroom interaction, learners are not free to self-select but must wait for turns allocated by the teacher. When nominated to speak, they must try to make the most of their opportunity – they might not get another chance. This means that they do not have extensive practice in managing turn-taking in the foreign language and, therefore, experience great difficulties in free discourse in organizing what they intend to convey in appropriate sequences of successive utterances.

Furthermore, research has shown that, generally, learners use only a narrow range of speech acts, mostly restricted to referential/informative language, while they hardly ever use the directive and expressive language functions. It can therefore be anticipated that learners will experience problems when having to use these functions in actual communication. In the present paper, learners' mastery of one particular communicative function, the request, is the object of investigation.

The communicative act of requesting has received much attention in the fields of philosophy and linguistics. Empirical studies, including a number of cross-cultural studies, have provided data on adult requestive behaviour, as well as data on the young child's acquisition of directive functions (see Trosborg (in preparation) for references). The request has also been the object of investigation in L_2 acquisition research. However, the empirical research on L_2 acquisition has been based mainly on written data elicited by means of questionnaires and discourse completion tests (an exception is the Bochum project, see Edmonson, *et al.,* 1984). Besides, little interest has been taken in the interactional process itself, even though the importance of conversational analysis for a thorough understanding of speech act behaviour has been emphasized (see Levinson, 1983).

Research findings built on spoken language as evidence of native requestive behaviour, rather than on written versions of intended speech, as well as research throwing light on learners' problems in mastering requests in actual communication situations, are of great importance for syllabus design and the development of communication tasks.

1.2. The speech act request

A request is an illocutionary act whereby a speaker (requester) conveys to a hearer (requestee) that he/she wants him/her to perform an act which is for the benefit of the speaker. The act may be a request for *non-verbal* goods and services, i.e. a request for an object, an action or some kind of service, etc., or it can be a request for *verbal* goods and services, i.e. a request for information.

The desired act is to take place post-utterance, either in the immediate future ('requests-now') or at some later stage ('requests-then') (see Edmonson and House, 1981:99). Thus the speech act of a request can be characterized as *pre-event,* in contrast to, for example, complaints, which are post-event in that they concern an offensive action which took place prior to the verbal act of complaining.

In the present study, the speech act request is taken to comprise all acts with the illocutionary point of 'getting somebody to do something' which range in illocutionary force from ordering to begging.

1.2.1. The request as an impositive act

When the requester wants somebody to do him/her a favour, this is generally at the cost of the requestee. The requester imposes on the requestee in some way when demanding a good or service. Impositive speech acts have been defined by Haverkate (1984:107) as 'speech acts performed by the speaker to influence the intentional behaviour of the hearer in order to get the latter to perform, primarily for the benefit of the speaker, the action directly specified or indirectly suggested by the proposition'.

The degree with which the requester intrudes on the requestee, called *degree of imposition,* may vary from small favours to demanding acts.

However, a speaker who tries to impinge on the behaviour of the hearer may do so for other reasons than to perform acts that are 'primarily to the benefit of the speaker', and in this respect, the request can be distinguished from other acts in which the speaker tries to exert his/her influence over the hearer.

1.2.2 The request as a face-threatening act

The notion of face is derived from Goffman (see e.g. Goffman, 1972) and further developed by Brown and Levinson (1978, 1987). The notion ties in with the English folk term of 'losing face' in the sense of being embarrassed or humiliated; it acknowledges politeness as ritual, and maintaining 'face' in interaction is the central element in commonly accepted notions of politeness.

As pointed out by Goffman (1972), a speaker is oriented towards both his/her own and his/her interlocutor's face, exhibiting a defensive orientation towards saving his/her own face and a protective orientation towards saving that of the interlocutor.

Face is emotionally determined and can 'be lost, maintained, or enhanced, and must be constantly attended to in interaction' (Brown and Levinson, 1987:61). People can be expected to defend their faces if threatened, and when defending their own faces they are likely to threaten other people's faces in turn. Therefore, it will in general be to the mutual interest of the participants to maintain each other's faces, and they can be expected to cooperate in maintaining face in interaction (ibid., p. 61).

The notion of face is claimed to be universal, but it is subject to cultural specification and elaboration in any particular society (see Brown and Levinson, 1987:13ff).

Brown and Levinson treat the aspects of face as 'basic wants' and distinguish between positive and negative face (ibid., p. 62):

negative face: the want of every 'competent adult member' that his actions be unimpeded by others

positive face: the want of every member that his wants be desirable to at least some others.

The speaker making a request attempts to exercise power or direct control over the intentional behaviour of the hearer, and in doing so threatens the requestee's negative face (his/her want to be unimpeded) by indicating that he/she does not intend to refrain from impeding the requestee's freedom of action. The requester also runs the risk of losing face him/herself, as the requestee may choose to refuse to comply with his/her wishes.

A requester has recourse to a wide variety of illocutionary strategies, some of which are indirect and can be used to save both his/her own and the interlocutor's face.

2. Experimental design

2.1. Request strategies

When issuing a request, various options are available to the addresser. Within the theory of Brown and Levinson (ibid.), the directive can be expressed 'off record', i.e. with no explicit directive force, or 'on record', i.e. with explicit directive force. In the case of the latter, the speaker can voice the directive with or without face redress in terms of mitigating devices. Table 1 gives a list of directives presented at levels of increasing directness. In the case of unmodified imperatives and unhedged performative utterances, the directive is phrased explicitly without face redress and serves as an order. Likewise, modals as *must* and *have to* are employed to impose a high degree of obligation on the addressee. Face-redress, on the other hand, can be obtained by using conventionally indirect directives, either in the form of 'hearer-oriented' questions concerning the ability/willingness of the addressee to perform a certain action, e.g. by employing the modals *can/could*, *will/would*, by 'permission statements' (employing the modals *may/might*, *can/could*), or by 'speaker-based' *want*-statements expressing the addresser's desires and needs. Finally, directives can be performed indirectly with no explicit marker of the impositive intent (i.e. 'off record').

For previous classifications of directive strategies which build on Austin's (1962) and Searle's (1969, 1976) theories, see Ervin-Tripp (1976), House and Kasper (1981), Brown and Levinson (1987), Trosborg (1987) and Blum-Kulka *et al.* (1989).

2.2. Modality markers

In addition to the selection of directness level, it is possible to soften, or increase, the impact a request strategy is likely to have on the requestee by modulating the request. There are various devices used for this purpose

REQUEST STRATEGIES, presented at levels of increasing directness.

Situation: Speaker requests to borrow Hearer's car.

I INDIRECT REQUESTS

    1. Hints   (mild)   I have to be at the airport in half an hour.

                    (strong)   My car has broken down.
                                   Will you be using your car tonight?

II HEARER-BASED CONDITIONS

    2. Ability   Could you lend me your car?

       Willingness   Would you lend me your car?

       Permission   May I borrow your car?

    3. Suggestory formulae   How about lending me your car?

III SPEAKER-BASED CONDITIONS

    4. Statement of wishes   I would like to borrow your car.

    5. Statement of desires and needs   I want/need to borrow your car.

IV DIRECT REQUESTS

    6. Statement of obligation   You must/have to lend me your car.

    7. Performatives (hedged)   I would like to ask you to lend me your car.

                    (unhedged)   I ask/require you to lend me your car.

    8. Imperatives   Lend me your car.

    9. Elliptical phrases   Your car (please).

Table 1: Request strategies

referred to as 'modality markers' (see House and Kasper, 1981). These are markers which either tone down the impact an utterance is likely to have on the hearer, called *downgraders*, or which have the opposite effect of increasing the impact, called *upgraders*. In connection with requests, it is clearly the former which are particularly relevant.

2.2.1. Downgraders

A requester who wants to mitigate his/her request has access to syntactic mitigating devices (syntactic downgraders), or he/she can include lexical/phrasal downgraders in the request (see Table 2).

Question	*Can you* hand me the paper?
Past tense	*Could* you hand me the paper?
Negation	*Couldn't* you hand me the paper?
Tag question	Hand me the paper, *will you?* Answer the 'phone, *won't you?* Could you do that for me, *okay?*
Modal verb	You *might* be able to help me.
Embedding + *'if'-clause*	*I'd be grateful if* you'd hand me the paper. *I'd really appreciate it if* you'd help me out.
Politeness marker	Hand me the paper, *please.*
Uncertainty	*Perhaps* you could lend me your paper? Could you *possibly* hand me the paper? I *wonder/was wondering* if you'd give me a hand?
Consultative device	Maybe you wouldn't *mind* giving me a hand?
Personal opinion	*I think* you ought to go now. *I'm afraid* you'll have to be going now.
Understatement	Would you just wait *a second?* Could you spare me *a minute?* Could I have *just a spot of* sherry, please? Couldn't you lower the volume *just a little*, please?
Vagueness	Could you *kind of* put it off for a while? Couldn't you *sort of* forget the whole matter? Could you *somehow* find the time to see me next week?
Hesitation	I *er, erm, er* - I wonder if you'd *er* ...

Table 2: Examples of downgraders
(adapted from Trosborg and McVeigh, 1988:32-33)

2.3. The data

The data are part of a corpus (360 conversations) elicited in a variety of social situations in order to provide knowledge of the sociolinguistic competence of Danish learners of English as compared to native speakers. The conversations involve various communicative acts. For the present paper, the data were elicited by means of role plays constructed on the basis of anticipated illocutionary acts of requesting.[1] The participants were video-taped in dyadic face-to-face conversations lasting approximately five minutes. The role relationships between the two participants varied along two parameters: 'dominance' and 'social distance'. With regard to dominance, the role relationship between the two participants was specified by either the authority or the lack of authority of one interactant over the other. The interactants either knew each other or had never met before (social distance). The following three types of role constellations were used:

(a) status unequals, non-intimates   + dominance
    (authority figures/subordinates)   + social distance

(b) status equals, non-intimates   - dominance
    (strangers)   + social distance

(c) status equals, intimates   - dominance
    (friends or near acquaintances)   - social distance

It was hypothesized that the addition of these parameters would result in situations demanding different levels of politeness.

The aim of the research was to obtain dialogues which were as spontaneous and natural as possible. Therefore, the distinction between (a) role playing and (b) role enactment (McDonough, 1981:80) was kept in mind when the role play material was constructed. The two types are characterized as follows: (a) 'pretending to react as if one were someone else in a different situation' and (b) 'performing a role that is part of one's normal life or personality'. The role enactment approach was considered the more advantageous, which meant that the role plays had to be tailor-made to the participants or, at least, contain problems and characters which were known beforehand to be familiar to those involved. This would facilitate the process for the foreign-langauge learners considerably, especially if they were unused to performing in this kind of exercise. Twelve concrete situations from everyday life (private life, at work, in public places, etc.) were chosen and role descriptions constructed. Typically, these descriptions involved some interactional complexity in the form of some kind of conflict or social difficulty that was not easily handled in a pre-patterned or routinized manner.

Three groups of learners and two groups of native speakers provided the data:[2]

Group I: Danish learners of English (intermediate level)
Group II: Danish learners of English (lower advanced level)
Group III: Danish learners of English (higher advanced level)
NS-E: Native speakers of English
NS-D: Native speakers of Danish

For groups I, II, III and NS-E, the requestee was always a native speaker of English.

The roles were distributed so that twelve subjects from each of the five groups were video-recorded in two different role constellations (a+b, or b+c, or a+c), viz. 24 situations, eight in each of three different role constellations, for each of the five groups, yielding a total of 120 conversations.

3. Results

120 conversations were analysed for the occurrence of request strategies, and the observed request strategies were classified according to the outlined levels of directness. In addition, the use of 'internal modification' (modality markers) and 'external modification' (supportive moves) were noted and classified. Finally, the influence on performance of the two parameters 'dominance' and 'social distance' was analysed. For the present purpose, the focus is on the use of request strategies.

Learner performance is compared to the performance of native speakers of English (NS-E), just as the requestive behaviour of the English informants is compared to that of their Danish counterparts (NS-D). Pragmatic deviances in learners are discussed with regard to possible interference from the mother tongue.

3.1. Total number of strategies

The total numbers of request strategies, observed for each group of informants, are presented in Table 3. It appears that NS-E used the largest number of strategies (3.5 request strategies as an average per conversation), followed by NS-D (2.5), while Group I and Group II learners had the lowest quantity of strategies (1.8). For Group III the ratio was 2.2.

	Group I	Group II	Group III	NS-E	NS-D
Total number of strategies	44	44	53	83	61
Average per conversation	1.8	1.8	2.2	3.5	2.5

Table 3: Total number of strategies

This result points to a shortcoming in learners in rephrasing their requests when these were not granted by the interlocutor. NS-E reformulated their requests twice as often as Group I and Group II learners. For Group III learners, as compared with the two less proficient groups, an increase was observed in the frequency with which a request was reformulated.

NS-D were less persistent in rephrasing their requests than NS-E, but more persistent than any of the three groups of learners.

3.2. Classification of requests strategies according to directness levels

3.2.1. Overall performance

For each individual conversation, the obtained request strategies were classified as belonging to one of the eight sub-categories outlined above.

When the directness levels selected by the three groups of learners were compared with the choices made by NS-E, statistically significant deviances were found for Strategy 1 (hints) and for Strategy 2 (preparatory). Both Group II and Group III learners produced significantly fewer hints than NS-E (p = 0.007, p = 0.010, respectively), and Group I learners fell short in their performance of Strategy 2 (p = 0.005).

No significant differences in the choices of directness levels were found when the performance of the two groups of native speakers were compared.

3.2.2. Relative distribution of the four major categories of request strategies

An analysis of the relative frequency of the four major categories of request strategies was performed, and the obtained percentages for each of the five groups are presented in Table 4.

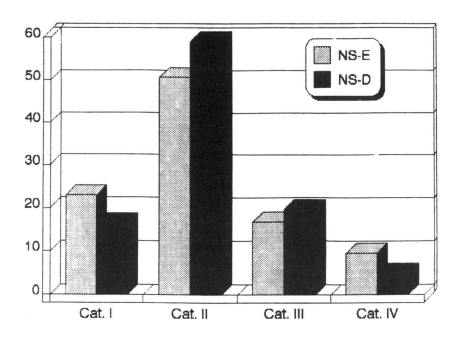

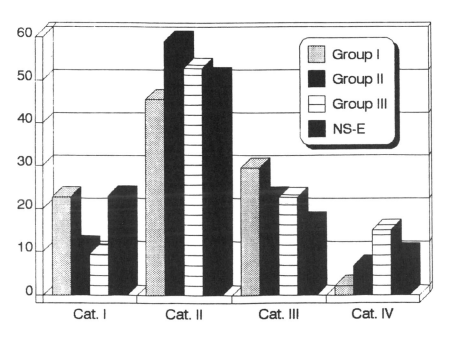

Table 4: Request strategies: Distribution of Categories I-IV in percentages

A statistical analysis was performed to determine the significance of the differences across the four major categories for each group of informants, and the pattern Category II : Category I, Category III and Category IV, respectively, was observed for all groups except Group I. Group I only used Category II significantly more often than Category IV. An over-representation of Category III (sincerity), counterbalanced by an under-representation of Category IV (direct request), was observed.

A similar pattern for Category II and Category III was observed for Group II. This group used Category III significantly more often than Category IV, and their performance showed an underuse of Category IV. In contrast, Group III learners overused this category.

Thus the data point to a less stable preference for Category II (preparatory) in the group of lowest proficiency, coupled with an overuse of Category III (sincerity). This overuse of Category III is also observed in the more advanced groups (II and III). Group I and Group II underuse Category IV (direct request), Group II less so than Group I. This underuse has turned to overuse in Group III learners. Both Group II and Group III learners tend to underuse Category I (hints).

The performance of NS-D differed significantly from that of NS-E only on Category IV, for which category the performance was significantly lower for NS-D. This difference may explain the observed underuse of this category in Groups I and II. Group III learners, who, evidently, are aware of the more frequent use of this category in English compared to Danish, deviate from NS-E by using this category too often.

Space does not permit presentation of the detailed results for all categories, but the following discussion of Categories I and II is representative of the analysis which can be made from the transcripts.

Notation: RL: Learner as requester
              RNS: Native speaker as requester
              NS: Native speaker as requestee

              Sociopragmatic categories:

              a-situation: request to authority figure
              b-situation: request to stranger
              c-situation: request to friend

3.3. Indirect strategies - Category I, Hints

The proportion of hints used by NS-E amounted to 22.9% of the total number of request strategies employed by this group. The proportion observed in Group I learners was very similar, 22.7% of the total number of strategies observed, whereas Group II and Group III learners had a significantly lower proportion of these strategies, 11.3% and 9.4%, respectively.

The lower proportion of hints in Group II and III learners was not surprising. Making an indirect request in the form of a hint implies a distance from what is said to what is actually meant, and this gap is to be breached by an inference process on the part of the requester, as well as on the part of the recipient of the request. The complexity of this process depends on the length of the path connecting the illocutionary act to the illocutionary goal, but normally, a more complex planning process would be required for the production of a hint than for a conventionally indirect or a direct request.

The finding that the proportion of hints in Group I learners equalled NS-E performance was unexpected, and an explanation is needed. It is suggested here that a number of these hints are qualitatively different from the hints produced by adult native speakers.

When given the task of making a request, these learners often got no further than stating the preliminaries in terms of describing their situation, while the request itself was not formulated. However, a statement of their conditions often made it possible for their native interlocutors to infer their intention. Consider the following extracts:

Extract 1. Situation: A baby-sitter requests to be exempted from her commitment (a)

RL: I've got a ticket to a concert tomorrow and eh my boyfriends get very disappointed if I don't come. (Group II)

What could have been part of a preparation for a request became the requester's turn as such with no subsequent requests.

Compare a similar preparation followed by a conventionally indirect request produced by an advanced learner:

Extract 2. Situation: The same as in Extract 1

RL: Well – eh – I've come to ask you something – because I know I'm supposed to start tomorrow night – babysitting

NS: Yes.

RL: but, you see, my boyfriend Tony just phoned me and said he had – some tickets for a Three Degrees concert in Albert Hall tomorrow night – so – I would like to ask you if I could get the night off? (Group III).

The 'hints' described above (Extracts 1 and 2) can be compared to utterances made by young children. Ervin-Tripp has observed that young children who at first do not have a well-articulated sense of what they have to do to relieve discomfort simply state their conditions and leave it up to their caretakers to find a solution (1967:42):

My nose is bleeding. (2.6)

I am hungry. (2.11)

Furthermore, it must be pointed out that some of the hints produced by learners appear very abrupt and impolite. The fact that the requester leaves it up to the hearer to specify or infer what is to be done may result in abruptness and even rudeness if the hint is not adequately prepared for, e.g.

Extract 3. Situation: Getting a coffee machine to England (a)

RL: I shall – I shall not eh the – eh I heard that you should er — take eh over to England.

NS: Ehm yes I'm returning

RL: Yes.

NS: tomorrow morning.

RL: Yeah - then here is my coffee machine. (Group I)

In Extract 3 the requester impolitely presumes that the requestee is willing to perform the desired act.

3.4. Hearer-based conditions - Category II, Preparatory

A strong preference for Category II was observed in all groups of informants. Half the total number of strategies fell in this category for NS-E (50.6%). Group III learners performed similarly to NS-E (52.8%). For Group I learners the percentage of Category II strategies was lower (45.5%), while for Group II learners the proportion was somewhat higher (59.1%) than that observed in NS-E.

Thus all learners recognized the importance of preparatory conditions in requestive behaviour. The choice of this strategy was no doubt greatly facilitated by the even stronger preference for these strategies in Danish (59.0%).

The preference for hearer-based preparatory conditions is not difficult to explain. This category involves more effective ways of requesting than Category I, as the desired act is explicitly mentioned and the hearer is the intended agent. At the same time, a high degree of politeness can be expressed.

The requester questions or otherwise refers to a preparatory condition decisive for the successful performance of the request and thus allows the requestee the option of politely refusing by referring to the condition in question. The requestee also has the opportunity of confirming one condition, while pointing to some other condition which is not fulfilled, as in the following example:

A: Would you like to come with us to the cinema tonight?

B: Sure, I would like to very much, but unfortunately, I can't. I've promised to baby-sit at our neighbours' house.

When employing a preparatory condition the requester also exhibits a protective orientation towards his/her own face, in that he/she does not take compliance for granted.

In addition, this category of request form allows extensive inclusion of modality markers. Most of the downgraders detailed above (p. 102) can be included, and extensive use of embedding is possible. Some examples follow:

Extract 4. Situation: Asking for removal help (b)

RNS: Well, yeah, well, you see, the thing was I wanted to ask you if you could if you could sort of help me lift the desk up to the second floor.

Extract 5. Situation: Getting a coffee machine to England (a)

RNS: I thought that perhaps I could eh, perhaps if you would mind taking something to Manchester for me.

The downgraders employed in Extract 4 are hesitators (*Well, yeah, well*, the cajoler (*you see*), the past tense (*was, wanted, could, could*, embedded *if*-clause, and a hedge (*sort of*). In Extract 5 the requester makes use of the past tense (*thought, could, would*), the downtoner (*perhaps, perhaps*), hesitation (*eh*), *if*-clause, and a consultative device (*mind*).

Consequently, the choice of these strategies affords the requester the possibility of lowering his/her expectations to the outcome of the request considerably, which reduces the discrepancy between what he/she wants to achieve and what would be regarded as good manners.

For the above mentioned reasons, strategies referring to hearer-based preparatory conditions are polite in most situations, and they are particularly appropriate in the request situations of the present study, which involved a high degree of imposition.

However, as the degree of politeness of a request is determined not only by the selection of directness level, but also by the inclusion of appropriate downgrading devices, the learners' choice of preparatory strategy, which in many situations would constitute an appropriate choice of directness level, did not necessarily ensure polite requestive behaviour. Lack of internal modification in the form of mitigating devices would often set off the learners' requests as being less polite than those put forward by NS-E. Consider the following learner requests:

Extract 6. Situation: Invitation (b)

RL: Do you want to eat with me – on eh Rose and Crown. (Group I)

Extract 7. Situation: The same as in Extract 4

RL: and ahm I eh if you could help me to move a big writing desk. (Group II)

With no preliminary preparators or softeners, the above requests appear abrupt and impolite, even though the hearer's willingness/ability is questioned.

3.5. Other categories

Category III, speaker-based sincerity conditions, was employed by all groups of speakers. It amounted to 16.9% of the total number of responses for NS-E, and to 19.7% for NS-D. Learners tended to use this category more frequently than native speakers, for Group II and III learners 22.7% and 22.6%, respectively. For Group I, who made the widest use of this category, it amounted to 29.5% of the total number of responses. Both Group I and Group II used this category significantly more often than direct requests. As for the use of sub-categories, both NS-E and NS-D used Strategy 4 about twice as often as Strategy 5. Group I and II learners also showed a preference for Strategy 4, whereas Group III learners had an equal number of responses on each strategy. NS-E made use of expressions like *I would like to, I'm eager to, I need*, etc., whereas only learners employed the expression *I want to*, which is less polite. A difference in sequential organization was also observed. Learners would use this type of request strategy as an initial strategy, which is likely to be impolite, in particular, if the request is issued upward in rank and compliance cannot be expected.

Direct requests are typically used when compliance is expected, either because the requester is superior in rank to the requestee, or because the favour asked carries a low degree of imposition. In situations involving an emergency and where an agreement has already been reached, the use of direct requests are also appropriate (see for example Trosborg and McVeigh, 1988). The social role constellations were specified so that the requester and the requestee were either of equal rank, or the requestee was superior in rank to the requester. The proportion of direct requests was therefore expected to be low in the data pertaining to native speakers. This expectation was confirmed. Only 9.6% of the requests produced by NS-E fell in this category.

However, even though NS-E favoured less direct strategies when expressing their impositive intent, direct requests were part of their requestive behaviour as well. For Group I learners, in particular, but also for Group II, an underuse of direct requests strategies was observed. Group I learners only used direct requests with a frequency of 2.3% of the total number of request strategies, while the frequency of Group II amounted to 6.8%. In contrast, Group III learners overused this category (15.1%) compared to NS-E norms.

The reported underuse of Category IV in Group I and Group II learners may be due to L_1 interference, as native speakers of Danish tended to avoid this category and only used it with a frequency of 4.9%.

When the total number of downgraders employed by each group of learners (calculated for each learner individually) was compared with the results for NS-E, a shortage of downgraders in learners reaching a high degree of significance was found. No significant differences between NS-E and NS-D were observed. Table 5 shows the number of downgraders used as an average per request strategy for the five groups of informants. For an account of the use of individual markers, see Trosborg (in preparation).

Group I	Group II	Group III	NS-E	NS-D
1.9	2.4	2.2	3.2	3.3

Table 5: Frequency of downgraders per request strategy

4. Summary and discussion

In conclusion, general tendencies in verbal requestive behaviour are summarized for Danish learners of English at three different proficiency levels and compared with verbal requestive behaviour in native speakers of English, for the purpose of accounting for the pragmatic difficulties experienced by Danish learners in mastering this speech act. An increase in the number of requests put forward in order to achieve desired goals was observed relative to increasing linguistic competence only for Group III learners.

Although advanced learners of English do become more persistent in their production of requests, they still produce far fewer requests than NS-E. This reluctance in Danish learners of English to reformulate their requests is likely to be due to pragmatic difficulties, as well as to L_1 interference.

With regard to the selection of directness levels, all three groups of learners showed a clear preference for Strategy 2 (preparatory), and they were thus in agreement with NS-E in acknowledging the need for polite request formulations required by the situational constraints. A high frequency of this category in Danish is likely to have resulted in positive transfer of these strategies. The overuse of direct strategies observed in German learners of English (House and Kasper, 1981) is not a pervading feature of requestive behaviour in Danish learners of English. On the contrary, Group I (in particular) and Group II learners produced fewer direct strategies than NS-E, and only Group III learners produced more direct strategies than NS-E, a tendency which did not reach statistical significance.

The selection of too direct strategies in German learners' English interlanguage can therefore be ascribed to L_1 interference. German learners of English are likely to experience greater difficulties in adjusting their interlanguage requests to NS-E norms than Danish learners of English. Whereas a change in the selection of directness level was demanded for the German learner in order to meet NS-E norms, the Danish learner could transfer the directness level he/she would have used in the mother tongue to a much larger extent and still express his/her intention at an appropriate level of directness. Thus the directness levels typically selected by NS-D greatly facilitated an approximation to NS-E norms in Danish learners of English as compared to German learners of English.

The lack of indirect strategies (Strategy 1, hints) in Group II and Group III learners points to a shortcoming in learners in employing mitigating devices, a tendency which finds further evidence in the learners' underuse of downgraders in their request strategies.

Surprisingly, Group I learners performed on a par with NS-E as far as the observed quantity of hints is concerned. However, on closer examination some of these hints appeared to be qualitatively different from hints produced by NS-E. Pragmatic shortcomings seemed to make these learners hesitate in realizing their pragmatic intent and thus prevented them from going 'on-record' and producing a transparent request. Preparation of a request, for example in terms of a statement of a problem, was often enough for NS-E to infer the learner's requestive intention, for which reason it functioned as a hint, even though this might not have been the original intention of the speaker.

The observed under-representation of direct requests (Strategy 8) in Group I, in particular, may have been caused by a reluctance in learners to express themselves in very direct terms in a foreign language. Fear of appearing impolite is likely to have resulted in exclusion of these strategies also in situations in which they could have been appropriately used. A similar reluctance to use direct strategies has been observed in English learners of Hebrew (Blum-Kulka, 1983).

Group III learners, who seemed to have overcome this fear, went in the opposite direction and produced slightly more direct strategies than NS-E.

The underuse of direct requests strategies in Group I learners, and to some extent in Group II learners as well, was outweighed by an overuse of speaker-based sincerity strategies (Strategy 4 and Strategy 5). Only learners employed the verb *want* when expressing their desires, a realization avoided completely by NS-E.

Learners' problems in adjusting requestive behaviour according to the socio-pragmatic constraints of the situation was a general trend in the present findings on learner behaviour. Learners experience difficulties in varying their behaviour in accordance with the involved social variables, and they generally lack the ability to differentiate their behaviour according to the involved social parameters (see Trosborg, in preparation).

No significant differences were observed in the quantity of downgraders employed by NS-E and NS-D, so the shortcomings in Danish learners cannot be directly ascribed to mother tongue interference due to a shortage in the use of these phenomena in the Danish language compared to the English. Other reasons for this pragmatic difficulty must be considered.

Differences in realization patterns in the two languages further complicated the transfer of mitigating devices from Danish to English. Even though the same categories of downgraders are fundamental to internal request modification in both languages, the means through which the individual downgraders are used in each language are somewhat specific to that particular language.

One-word structures in Danish might be realized as a phrase consisting of several items in English, and vice versa. What in one language is incorporated in the request structure might in the other language appear as a pre- or post-positioned modifier. A downgrader may be realized by syntactic means in one language, and by lexical/phrasal markers in another, etc.

Thus, in a number of cases a direct word-to-word translation of a downgrader was not possible, and a restructuring was necessary in order to convey the intended meaning in the target language, as in the examples presented below.

Whereas the English politeness marker *please* typically appears in pre- or post-position to a request, the Danish equivalent is incorporated in the verb phrase, either by means of the phrase *være så venlig* (*be so kind*), or by the selection of the verb *bede om* (ask politely) used mainly upward in rank, e.g.

(210)   Would you close the door, *please*.
        Vil du/De *være så venlig* at lukke døren.

(211)   Could I have a cake, *please*?
        Må jeg *bede om* en kage.

114

Within the light of the present findings, it can be concluded that, on the whole, learners were less well prepared, less polite and less persuasive, and consequently less successful in their requestive behaviour, than their English speaking counterparts.

The shortcomings in sociolinguistic competence and the inferior discourse competence in learners pointed out above may be an artifact of classroom practice. It is my hope that studies like the present one may highlight the need for the development of sociopragmatic skills in L_2 learners.

Notes

1. The elicitation material consists partly of role plays from Edmonson *et al.* (1984) and partly of new role plays.
2. Group I learners came from secondary school, 9th grade, and from business school, level 2; Group II learners from *gymnasium*, 2nd year, and from business school, level 3; and Group III learners from the University of Aarhus, 4th semester, and from the Aarhus School of Business, 4th semester.

References

Austin, John L. 1962. *How to Do Things with Words*. New York: Oxford University Press.

Blum-Kulka, Shoshana. 1983. 'Interpreting and performing speech acts in a second language: A cross-cultural study of Hebrew and English', in Wolfson, N. and Judd, E. (eds.), *Sociolinguistics and Language Acquisition*. Rowley, Mass.: Newbury House.

Blum-Kulka, Shoshana, House, Juliane and Kasper, Gabriele. 1989. *Cross-cultural Pragmatics. Requests and Apologies*. Norwood: Ablex Publishing Corporation.

Brown, Penelope and Levinson, Stephen C. 1978. 'Universals in language usage: Politeness phenomena', in Goody, E.N. (ed.), *Questions and Politeness*. Cambridge: Cambridge University Press.

Brown, Penelope and Levinson, Stephen S. 1987. *Politeness: Some Universals in Language Use*. Cambridge: Cambridge University Press.

Edmondson, Willis and House, Juliane. 1981. *Let's Talk and Talk About It*. München: Urban and Schwarzenberg.

Edmondson, Willis, House, Juliane, Kasper, Gabriele and Stemmer, Brigitta. 1984. 'Learning the pragmatics of discourse: A project report', *Applied Linguistics* 5, pp. 113-127.

Ervin-Tripp, Susan. 1976. 'Is Sybil there? The structure of some American English directives', *Language in Society* 5/1, pp. 25-66.

Goffman, Erving. 1972. 'On face-work: An analysis of ritual elements in social interaction', in Laver, John and Hytcheson, Sundy (eds.), *Communication in Face-to-face Interaction*. Harmondsworth: Penguin, pp. 319-346.

Haverkate, Henk. 1984. *Speech Acts, Speakers and Hearers*. Pragmatics and Beyond, vol 4. Amsterdam: John Benjamins Publishing Company.

House, Juliane and Kasper, Gabriele. 1981. 'Politeness markers in English and German', in Coulmas, Florian (ed.), *Conversational Routine*. The Hague: Mouton.

Levinson, Stephen C. 1983. *Pragmatics*. Cambridge: Cambridge University Press.

Loercher, Wolfgang. 1986. 'Conversational structures in the foreign language classroom', in Kasper, Gabriele (ed.), *Learning, Teaching and Communication in the Foreign Language Classroom*. Aarhus: Aarhus University Press.

Long, Michael H. and Porter, Patricia A. 1985. 'Group work, interlanguage talk and second language acquisition', *TESOL Quarterly* 19, pp. 207-28.

McDonough, Steven H. 1981. *Psychology in Foreign Language Teaching*. London: George Allen and Unwin.

Searle, John R. 1969. *Speech Acts*. Cambridge: Cambridge University Press.

Searle, John R. 1976. 'The classification of illocutionary acts', *Language in Society* 5, pp. 1-24.

Trosborg, Anna. 1984. 'Language learning in formal and informal contexts', *IRAAL*, Dublin.

Trosborg, Anna, 1988. 'Request strategies in natives/non-natives', paper presented at Second Language Research Forum, Honolulu.

Trosborg, Anna, in preparation. *Interlanguage Pragmatics*. Unpublished dissertation.

Trosborg, Anna and McVeigh, Jean, 1988. *Rules and Roles - A Workbook in Communication*. Gjellerup: Systime.

Sex, Status and Style in the Interview

Don Porter and Shen Shu Hung

1. Introduction

The notion that people adjust their L_1 speech in a systematic manner, depending on who they are talking to, and when, is at the root of sociolinguistics, and has long been with us (e.g. Malinowski, 1935; Firth, 1950). The search for relevant variables participating in this systematic variation in the speech situation has therefore formed an important strand of sociolinguistic research, and more recently of applied linguistics and specifically foreign language testing research. Thus Farhady (1982) considered variation of learners' linguistic performance in relation to their sex, university status (graduate or undergraduate), major field of study, and nationality. Shohamy (1983) considered whether learners' spoken language varied significantly with changes in 'speech style' (reporting the content of a lecture *versus* interacting in an interview), topic, and level of experience in the interviewer. Spurling and Ilyin (1985) investigated linguistic variation in relation to learners' educational background, language background, and age. The framework proposed by Weir and Bygate (1990) for defining tasks assessing spoken language interaction suggests that the nature and quality of language produced will vary with a number of dimensions of variable, one dimension being features of the interlocutor(s). These features will include, amongst other things, the sex and relative status of the interlocutor(s). This paper will seek to provide evidence that two variables significantly affect the assessment of spoken language by interview: the sex and status of the interviewer.

1.1. Sex of participants

While it is well known that many languages formally mark utterances according to the sex of the speaker and the addressee, it is only relatively recently that studies have been published of subtle linguistic features distinguishing male and female speech and distinguishing speech addressed to males and

117

females (although see Trudgill, 1973). Such sets of features are said to constitute different interactional styles.

It has often been reported in the literature (Zimmerman and West, 1975; Hirshmann, 1974; Fishman, 1978) that in mixed-sex interactions, male speakers often give few or delayed minimal responses ('mhm', 'yeah', 'mm', 'uhuh', etc.) when listening to another speaker, whereas female speakers produce such responses more frequently and more promptly, indicating active attention. The import to the speaker of the limited minimal responses of the male might well be to indicate lack of interest, or impatience to take over the turn himself, whereas the woman's responses would suggest solidarity with and support for the speaker (Coates, 1986; Graddol and Swann, 1989).

Lakoff (1975) suggested that women are perceived as expressing themselves in a more tentative way than men, and one of the ways in which this perception is encouraged is through use of tag-questions. Men and women do not differ significantly in the overall frequency with which they use tag questions in spoken interaction, but they do tend to use them differently: men tend to use them to express their own uncertainty, whereas women tend to use them affectively, expressing the user's attitude to, and thus facilitating, the addressee's contribution to the discourse. Such facilitative tag-questions, it is claimed, decrease the strength of assertions; the frequent use of such tags tends to ensure that spoken interaction proceeds smoothly.

Brown and Levinson (1978) describe a number of strategies for expressing politeness, one of which is to repeat part or all of what a previous speaker has said. Citing Brown and Levinson's work, Coates (1986) refers to women's tendency to express politeness and support by acknowledging and building on the utterances of other speakers in an interaction. We might therefore expect women to both repeat and expand on the utterances of other speakers in an interaction.

Cameron (1985) criticizes the exclusive or inappropriate use of male interviewers in sociolinguistic surveys, as their characteristic male speech style might well produce different effects on male and female interviewees.

The foreign/second language teaching literature also contains reports of research into differential performance of male and female learners. Thus Farhady (1982), examining the relationship between the linguistic performance of 800 foreign students entering UCLA, and the variables of students' sex, university status, major field of study, and nationality, found no significant linguistic difference between male and female students, except in listening comprehension.

Spurling and Ilyin (1985), investigating the effect on a battery of language tests of the learner variables of sex, length of stay in the United States, age, high-school graduation status, and language background, found that learners' sex and length of stay had no significant effect.

Such studies tend, however, to focus on the differential level of performance of male and female learners as groups, and do not consider the relative performance of males and females in interaction with each other. Neither does the foreign/second language teaching literature tend to reflect the detailed findings of L_1 research into the nature of male/female linguistic differences, nor does it echo the warnings of Cameron (1985) and others on the consequences of using interviewers of a given sex. Given the claimed facilitative nature of female speech characteristics (minimal responses, tag questions, etc.), one might expect that learners would produce superior performance in spoken language when being interviewed by women.

There have been a number of small investigations at Reading into the possible effects of the sex of participants in spoken language interaction, beginning with an M.A. project (Locke, 1984). In that very restricted study four male postgraduate Iraqi and Saudi students at Reading consistently performed at a higher level, based on two distinct sets of performance measures, when interviewed by males, than when interviewed by females. In a subsequent interview study involving 13 postgraduate Algerian life-science students (11 male, 2 female) (Porter, 1991), the sex of the interviewer, the general personality of the interviewer (more outgoing *versus* more reserved), and the acquaintanceship of the participants (interviewer known/unknown to interviewee) were systematically varied so that every student was interviewed twice: once by a male, once by a female; once by a more outgoing interviewer, once by a more reserved interviewer; once by someone known, once by someone unknown. Of these three variables, only the sex of the interviewer was associated with any significant difference of performance on two distinct sets of assessment criteria.

Both the above studies were concerned exclusively with Arab students. In a series of interviews conducted at Reading early in 1990, an attempt was made to replicate the Algerian study, but this time with a sample of students from a variety of cultures, and with a better balance of male and female students. Although the study was never completed, preliminary analysis suggested once again that there was a slight, though in this case insignificant, tendency for the sex of the interviewer to have an effect on the scores achieved by the interviewees.

In an attempt to shed some light on this point, the writers decided to test the following hypothesis:

1. In one-to-one interviews, learners from diverse national, cultural and linguistic backgrounds will achieve significantly higher scores when the interviewer is female than when the interviewer is male.

1.2. Status of participants

The relative social status of participants in L_1 spoken interaction has long been assumed to affect the language of the interaction, and research has produced appropriate evidence (e.g. Geertz, 1960; Labov, 1970). It is therefore not surprising that, eventually, it should at least be assumed that such a status effect would also occur in the L_2 speech of learners (Tarone, 1979; Wolfson, 1986). Nevertheless, evidence for a status effect on the language of L_2 learners is hard to come by.

There is moreover at least a possibility that any sex variable might be confounded with a status variable. It may well be that males in many societies are accorded higher status than women. Thus any attempt to determine whether the sex of participants is a relevant variable in spoken language assessment will need to confront the possibility that the relative status of participants will also – or instead – be a relevant variable. It will therefore be necessary to devise an experimental design which will tease these two variables apart.

In an attempt to shed some light on whether differences in the status of participants in oral interaction significantly affect the performance of learners, the writers decided to test the following hypothesis:

2. In one-to-one interviews, learners from diverse national, cultural and linguistic backgrounds will achieve significantly higher scores when the interviewer is presented so as to suggest relatively low status, than when the interviewer is presented so as to suggest relatively high status.

2. Method

2.1. Subjects

There were 50 participants in this study: 28 interviewees and 22 interviewers. The interviewees – 14 male and 14 female – were all students enrolled in language courses at the Centre for Applied Language Studies, University of Reading (CALS), during summer 1990. They came from 18 different countries with very different linguistic and cultural backgrounds: 16 came from Asia, 6 from Europe, 4 from Africa (including 1 Arab) and 2 from Latin America. They ranged in age from early twenties to early forties, the great majority coming within the mid-twenty to mid-thirty range. With the exception of three students who intended to continue with language courses, the students were about to enter postgraduate study in a wide variety of fields. Some of the students themselves had relatively high status from their professions in the home country, but this information was not systematically collected. All the students

120

were at an intermediate level of oral proficiency, though a few verged on advanced level while a few others were just above basic level.

The interviewers were all native speakers of English under the age of 35. Six were university lecturers, four were members of administrative staff who were used to dealing with students, and the remainder were teachers of English as a second or foreign language from different parts of the world, currently engaged in postgraduate studies at the Centre for Applied Language Studies. All of them had some experience of giving interviews.

2.2. Design

Each subject was interviewed twice, once by a male and once by a female. Each interviewer was presented once in 'boosted-status' mode, once in 'non-boosted status' (see below), such that each interviewee was interviewed by one interviewer in 'boosted status', one in 'non-boosted status'. The interviewers were instructed to ignore the manner in which they were introduced, and to simply 'be themselves' in each interview. To control for a possible order effect, the first interviewer was male in half of the interviews, and female in the other half. In order for the two interviews to be considered equivalent, the tasks in the interviews had to be as similar as possible, yet if boredom and fatigue were to be avoided, the tasks had to be different. The two tasks were therefore designed to be 'same-but-different'. Each interview lasted about 15 minutes, and took the form of the interviewer eliciting information from the interviewee in order to fill out three parts of a form with personal details of the student. The particular questions asked in the two interviews were, however, slightly different in content, requiring different replies. Each interview had a three-part structure: roughly four minutes of short turns, requiring very circumscribed pieces of information about the student's education and family; roughly four minutes of longer turns about the student's future career; and roughly four minutes of discussion designed to elicit information about the student's social background.

2.3. Procedure

Interviewees and interviewers were unknown to each other. Before the interview, they were told that the purpose of the experiment was to discover the factors affecting spoken language performance in interviews, and that the interviews would be videoed for future analysis; they were not, however, told the precise objectives of the study. All the interviews were conducted in a small meeting room in the Centre for Applied Language Studies.

The status of interviewers was 'boosted', or not, solely by the manner in which they were introduced to the student. When interviewers were introduced in 'boosted' mode, their name was given as Mr/Mrs/Ms/Dr plus family name, and a brief resume of their most important-sounding titles and responsibilities was given. The introducer did not smile during this process, and maintained some physical distance from the interviewer. Every effort was made to show great respect to the interviewer. On the other hand, when an interviewer was introduced with non-boosted status, the introducer stood close to the interviewer, and smiled as much as was compatible with being natural. In this mode the interviewer was introduced by first name only, was described as a friend (e.g. 'who sometimes helps us', 'an old student of mine' etc.), no resume of offices and responsibilities was recited, and at some stage in the proceedings a friendly pat on the arm or back was given.

2.4. Data analysis

The total corpus of data consisted of 56 fifteen-minute video-taped oral interviews, 28 of which had male interviewers, 28 female. Cutting across these two categories, 28 had interviewers with 'boosted' status, 28 'nonboosted'.

Each interviewee's spoken language performance was assessed twice and independently by a male and a female rater. A total of 9 raters were trained and used; some of these were already experienced raters, some were not.

Performance was rated using the Foreign Service Institute Supplementary Rating Scales (Oller, 1979). These scales consist of five separate measures (accent, grammar, vocabulary, fluency and comprehension), each with a range of six points to be awarded, and then differentially weighted. In addition, raters were asked two questions:

'Any comment on the student's performance?'

and

'If this is the second interview for this student, do you notice any particular differences not accounted for in the rating scale?'

t-tests were then conducted to compare students' mean scores for overall performance and for performance on individual measures when interviewed by males and females, and when the interviewer had 'boosted' and 'non-boosted' status.

3. Results

No significant difference was found between mean spoken language perform-ances in the two status conditions (p<.05), on any of the five individual rating scale measures or on the totals for these measures weighted in accordance with standard FSI procedures (Table 1). Hypothesis 2 had therefore to be rejected: there was no evidence that a difference in perceived status contributed to any marked difference in spoken language performance.

	'Non-boosted' status (28 interviewees)		'Boosted' status (28 interviewees)		
	Mean	SD	Mean	SD	t
Accent	2.12	.39	2.09	.39	1.36
Grammar	22.32	4.75	22.25	5.20	.20
Vocabulary	15.79	3.66	15.77	3.72	.08
Fluency	7.59	1.94	7.63	1.99	-.20
Comprehension	16.02	3.58	16.04	3.75	-.08
Total	**63.81**	**13.64**	**63.71**	**14.28**	**.038**

Table 1: Mean scores for spoken language with 'boosted' and 'non-boosted' status

Similarly, no significant difference was found (p<.05) on individual rating scale measures between mean scores achieved with male interviewers and mean scores achieved with female interviewers. However, when scores on the five measures were weighted and totalled in accordance with FSI procedures, there was a clear and significant (p<.05) tendency for higher scores to be achieved when the interviewer was a woman (Table 2). Our Hypothesis 1 was therefore supported on overall scores, but not for the individual measures of accent, grammar, vocabulary, fluency and comprehension: the overall scores indicated a significant tendency for female interviewers to elicit superior spoken language performance.

	Female interviewers (28 interviewees)		Male interviewers (28 interviewees)		
	Mean	SD	Mean	SD	t
Accent	2.11	.39	2.10	.38	.44
Grammar	22.46	4.91	22.11	5.05	1.01
Vocabulary	15.89	3.80	15.66	3.59	.84
Fluency	7.69	2.02	7.53	1.90	.93
Comprehension	16.18	3.54	15.88	3.79	1.40
Total	**64.35**	**13.86**	**63.18**	**14.04**	**1.73***

*$p < .05$

Table 2: Mean scores for spoken language with male and female interviewers

4. Discussion

This study went beyond those earlier studies which suggested a sex-of-interlocutor effect when the interviewees were from a common culture (Arab), and when they were exclusively or dominantly male (Porter, 1991). Those earlier studies were also characterised by the small number of interviewees participating. Here, interviewees were from 18 different countries on 4 continents, males and females were equal in number, and the number of interviewees rose to 28 (= 56 interviews).

A status-of-interlocutor effect was not to be found. It may be that the 'boosted'-'non-boosted' status distinction was not brought out sufficiently heavily in the introduction of interviewers for it to have a noticeable effect on interviewees' performance; or that in the context of an interview conducted by teachers and teachers' friends, in an academic institution, all interviewers were perceived as having relatively high status; or finally that interviewees saw through the experimenters' subterfuge when academic staff, teachers, etc. were presented as 'friends', 'students', etc. Nevertheless the lack of evidence for a status effect must lead us at most to bring in a verdict of 'not proven' on the suggestion that status and sex are confounded in the interviewer, and might conceivably point to status being an irrelevant interlocutor variable in the assessment of spoken language ability. Many variables may play a part here – more research will be needed to tease them apart.

On the other hand, significant sex-of-interviewer effect appeared to be clearly demonstrated, and thus appears to remain a significant variable in the interview. This is consistent with the findings of sociolinguistic research that the sex of participants plays an important role in conversational interaction, while going further to show that the sex of one participant in the interaction may elicit differential speech performance in another – at least in the context of the interview used for educational measurement.

It will be remembered from our review of the literature that male and female speakers of English L_1 are reported as employing different interactional styles, marked typically among females by a tendency towards greater use of minimal responses, repetitions, expansions and tag questions. We shall refer henceforth to the relatively frequent use of these features as 'female speech style', and the relatively infrequent use of these features as 'male speech style', regardless of the actual biological sex of the person speaking. The investigators felt that the difference in interviewee-performance might be related to male and female speech-style characteristics – either individually or taken together. Part of the data was therefore transcribed (the second minute of Part 1 of the interview, and the second minute of Part 2, from the first 28 interviews, 14 with male interviewers and 14 with female interviewers) and analysed for the purpose of comparing performances associated with possibly different male and female interviewer styles.

The transcriptions did indeed suggest evidence (Table 3) for differential use of some of these characteristics. Female interviewers produced significantly more minimal responses and expansions ($p<.01$) than male interviewers; tag questions occurred rarely in the speech of either sex, and repetitions occurred more frequently in the speech of female interviewers, but not significantly so. A small minority of the male interviewers displayed the characteristics of the typically female speech style, and a small minority of the female interviewers in their turn displayed the characteristics typical of male speech style.

Overall rating scale scores associated with female speech style features taken as a whole were significantly higher ($p<.01$) than scores associated with male speech style features (Table 4). In particular, students tended to achieve significantly higher grammar, vocabulary and comprehension scores in female speech style interviews. These features were also associated with marginally but not significantly higher fluency and comprehension scores. Accent was not affected by style.

Finally, in their responses to the two additional questions on the rating scales, raters frequently commented that students appeared to be more relaxed, and smiled more often, when interviewed by women. This observation rein-

	Female interviewers n = 14		Male interviewers n = 14		
	Mean	SD	Mean	SD	t
Minimal responses	12.28	5.14	7.00	3.09	2.93*
Repetitions	2.40	1.99	1.50	1.60	1.36
Expansions	2.40	1.45	.93	1.07	2.72*

*p<.01

Table 3: 'Female speech style' characteristics in male and female interviewers

	'Female' (14 interviewees)		'Male' (14 interviewees)		
	Mean	SD	Mean	SD	t
Grammar	20.86	4.85	19.79	4.41	1.82*
Vocabulary	14.64	3.24	13.71	2.85	3.04**
Fluency	6.77	1.75	6.64	1.20	.39
Comprehension	14.61	2.84	13.96	2.60	1.27*
Total (including accent)	**58.76**	**12.36**	**55.89**	**10.37**	**2.80****

*p<.05   **p<.01

**Table 4: Spoken language ratings in interviews with 'female' and 'male'
speech style characteristics**

forces the perceived supportive nature of female participation in spoken language interaction as reported in the sociolinguistic literature. It was noted, however, that one female Japanese student smiled more frequently when interviewed by a man, while the single Arab student, a male, though a fluent speaker, seemed to be more hesitant when interviewed by a woman. He remarked later that he felt uncomfortable with women. These last two cases suggest that, while the sex of the interviewer is likely to affect a student's performance, the nature of that effect – positive or negative – may be determined by the student's cultural background.

5. Conclusion

The warnings in the sociolinguistic literature against the exclusive use of male interviewers in sociolinguistic surveys have not been paralleled in the field of language testing. The findings of the study reported here, however, suggest that in the language testing interview context at least the sex of the interviewer is an important variable.

References

Brown and Levinson. 1978. 'Universals in language usage: politeness phenomena', in Goody, E.N., *Questions and Politeness Strategies in Social Interaction*. Cambridge: CUP.

Cameron, D. 1985. *Feminism and Linguistic Theory*. London: Macmillan.

Coates, J. 1986. *Women, Men and Language*. London: Longman.

Farhady, H. 1982. 'Measures of language proficiency from the learners' perspective', *TESOL Quarterly* 16.

Firth, J.R. 1950. 'Personality in language and society', *The Sociological Review* xlii/2.

Fishman, P.M. 1978. 'Interaction: the work women do', *Social Problems* 25.

Geertz, C. 1960. *The Religion of Java*. Free Press.

Graddol, D. and Swann, J. 1989. *Gender Voices*. Oxford: Basil Blackwell.

Hirshmann, L. 1974. 'Analysis of supportive and assertive behaviour in conversations', summarised in Thorne, B. and Henley, N., *Language and Sex: Difference and Dominance*. Rowley, Mass.: Newbury House, 1975.

Labov, W. 1970. *The Study of Language in its Social Context. Studium Generale* 23.

Lakoff, R. 1975. *Language and Woman's Place*. New York: Harper and Row.

Locke, C. 1984. Unpublished M.A. project. Reading University.

Malinowski, B. 1935. *Coral Gardens and their Magic*. London: Allen and Unwin.

Oller, J.W. Jr. 1979. *Language Tests at School*. London: Longman.

Porter, D. 1991. 'Affective factors in the assessment of oral interaction', *RELC Journal*.

Shohamy, E. 1983. 'The stability of oral proficiency assessment on the Oral Interview testing procedures', *Language Learning* 33.

Spurling, S. and Ilyin, D. 1985. 'The impact of learner-variables on language test performance', *TESOL Quarterly* 19.

Tarone, E. 1979. 'Interlanguage as chameleon', *Language Learning* 29.

Trudgill, P. 1973. 'Phonological rules and sociolinguistic variation in Norwich English', in Bailey, C-J.N. and Shuy, R.W. (eds): *New ways of Analyzing Variation in English.* Washington, D.C.: Georgetown University Press.

Weir, C. and Bygate, M. 1990. 'Meeting the criteria of communicativeness in a spoken language test'. Paper presented at the RELC 1990 Regional Seminar, Singapore.

Wolfson, N. 1986. 'Research methodology and the question of validity', *TESOL Quarterly* 20.

Zimmerman, D. H. and West, C. 1975. 'Sex roles, interruptions and silences in conversation', in Thorne, B. and Henley, N., *Language and Sex: Difference and Dominance.* Rowley, Mass.: Newbury House.

Teaching English to Children – an Activity-Based Approach

David Vale

A teacher using an activity-based course for the first time needs support and guidance. The approach is different. Many of the techniques and attitudes seem to conflict with traditional EFL methodology. On the other hand, language teachers with experience of teaching children realise that EFL methodology alone does not work with children. Indeed, it should be realised that, for the most part, EFL methodology and curricula have been developed by educators with little experience of teaching children – and for the purpose of teaching highly motivated adults. Teachers of English to children must look at the learning needs of *children*, and make sure that these needs are put first.

1. Priorities

The priority for teachers is to establish a working relationship with the children, and to encourage them to do the same with their classmates. The teacher's role is that of parent, teacher, friend, motivator, organiser. The necessary skills for these roles have more to do with understanding children's development, children's needs, children's interests, the children themselves, than with EFL methodology. Teachers need to focus on areas such as relationships, the provision of whole learning experiences (for the *whole* child), classroom organisation and learner motivation – rather than vocabulary, structure, functions, communicative practice and choral drills.

Young learners have specific learning needs. It is not sufficient to provide children, whether native or non-native speakers, with a programme of study which merely focuses on language, or indeed on any other isolated skill. Instead, it is necessary to offer a whole learning situation in which language development is an integral part of the learning taking place, and not the only end product. Moreover, it is impossible to know what children in any given language lesson can or will learn. What *is* known is that children learn best when they are involved. They learn best when they are the *owners* of their work –

129

when they have the opportunity to experience and experiment for themselves. This means *doing*. This means providing a range of child-centred activities.

Language activities for the sake of teaching language alone have little place in the children's classroom. For example, it is nonsense to ask children: *Is there a book on the table? Is there a lamp on the table?* where the purpose of these questions is merely to teach *there is*. Children simply do not learn language one structure or six new words at a time. They learn language whole, as part of a whole learning experience. It is the responsibility of teachers to provide this whole learning experience.

2. An activity-based curriculum

Children in a foreign language learning situation may only be studying English for two or three hours per week. In order to make the most use of the time available, teachers must have clear objectives. In an activity-based approach the relationship between the topics being studied and the language to be focused upon (or to be covered according to the school curriculum) can be clearly demonstrated. For example,[1] where the topic is measuring (*personal height, weight, ability to jump, hop, etc.*), Table 1 illustrates the relationship between the main activity (measuring) and the language.

The Children's Experience of Language *Input* across the Curriculum		Language *Output* from the Children in an Activity-Based Context		
Activities & Topics	Teacher's questions instructions, and comments about:	Vocabulary	*Physical Response* text	Expressions and Structures
Measuring & personal measurements	measuring distance, height, etc.; recording results of measuring	numbers 0-9 eye hair foot hand centimetres	stand up reach up stretch higher wider relax sit down	me her him Yes/no Verb *to be* *I'm...(1,4,2 centimetres), S/he's...*

Table 1

130

Similarly, Table 2 demonstrates this relationship for an art and craft topic that includes *making a beetle*.

The Children's Experience of Language *Input* across the Curriculum		Language *Output* from the Children in an Activity-Based Context		
Activities & Topics	Teacher's questions, instructions, and comments about:	Vocabulary	*Physical Response* text	Expressions and Structures
Beetles & Beetle games	making a beetle; playing beetle games; numbers; parts of the body	parts of the body numbers 21-30 long (longer) big (bigger) small (smaller) round dice a/the	draw... cut... glue... pick up... say...	my turn your turn her turn his turn Verb *to have:* *...has a* *(small round* *head, etc.)*

Table 2

In other words, not only are all the *language* needs of a traditional EFL curriculum being covered, but at the same time the children are being exposed to (and will acquire) a wide range of language as part of a whole learning experience *in English*.

3. A framework for teaching *in English*

Teachers using an activity-based approach for the first time have the support of a clearly defined teaching framework. The children are guided along a learning pathway which starts with input and active understanding, continues with hands-on experience, and ends in speaking. This *framework* consists of three learning (teaching) phases:

i. **A Preparation Phase** involving a series of *physical response* activities with the key language needed for the *Main Activity*. In this phase the children are exposed to key language, respond to it – but do not need to produce it.

ii. **A Main Activity Phase** in which the children complete a practical topic. In the first example above, the children complete a variety of *measuring* tasks and record their results. The topic is of value in *whole learning* terms, and is not merely a means of practising language. It encourages the children to find a practical context for the language they have already experienced, but cannot necessarily produce. The results of this hands-on experience create a natural text for the ensuing *follow up* phase.

iii. **A Follow-up Phase** in which the teacher uses the confidence and experience gained by the children in the two previous phases to encourage them to speak. During this stage the teacher focuses on specific language points. In the example of *measuring*, by using the *numbers* and *units* they have acquired, the children are able to say:

– how tall they are: *(I'm) one, four, two centimetres*
– how far they can reach: *one, six, nine centimetres*
– how far they can jump, hop, etc.

and respond to a variety of classroom questions and instructions that arise within the context of measuring:

T: *Who's the tallest in the class?*
S: *You.*
T: *Who's the shortest?*
S: *Maria.* etc.

Table 3 shows the teaching *framework* suggested for this topic.

Once this basic pattern for teaching and learning has been established in the classroom, it becomes possible to teach selected parts of the everyday curriculum, or of specific topics and projects – *in English.*

4. Putting the children's needs first

In the EFL classroom there is a lot of pressure on the teacher to produce immediate, tangible results:

– Teachers are concerned with their own performance.
– Children need to be heard to speak English by proud parents.
– Administrators need concrete evidence of progress.

As a result teachers tend to feel guilty if specific new structures and new words are not *learnt* every lesson. This is potentially a very harmful state of affairs. If teachers insist on this type of achievement from children, they will inevitably encourage failure. Young children have no defence against this sense of failure. Children who have tried their best and failed to produce the result the teacher wants will lose confidence and interest. They will feel, quite wrongly, that English is too difficult for them – and stop trying.

INPUT PHASE	HANDS-ON PHASE (Main Activity)		FOLLOW-UP PHASE
Lesson 1: Preparation activities	Lesson 2: Measuring activities (1)	Lesson 3: Measuring activities (2)	Lesson 4: Follow-up activities
Warm Up: play *Chinese whispers* or *pass the bean bag* for names	Warm Up: review and develop the *Action Game*. Use Class Cassette	Warm Up: develop the *Action Game*. Use Class Cassette	Warm Up: review and develop the *Action Game*. Use Class Cassette
Presenting New Language: numbers 0-9	Check Homework: check and display *photos*	Check Homework: record results on the board	Check Homework: Use Class Cassette
Introduce the physical response (*Action Game*) text. Use Class Cassette	Presenting New Language: *colours of eyes and hair*	Presenting New Language: *common classroom items*	Complete the *Workpage*. (Review and record activities)
Game: *stand on numbers* or *Twister* with numbers	Activity: children measure heights. Record results on class chart	Activity: measure jumps and hops. Record results on class chart	Language Practice: giving information about the results
Review: the children say how old they are	Language Practice: short, true answers about the results	Language Practice: short, true answers about the results	Homework: show parents the completed *Workpage*
Homework: bring in a passport photo	Homework: children measure other members of their families	Homework: complete and tidy up *results* page	Round Up: sing *One Little Indian*
Round Up: the children *make numbers* with their bodies	Round Up: writing numbers on partner's back	Round Up: sing *One Little Indian*. Use Class Cassette	

Table 3

Children must be allowed to learn at their own pace. Language learning targets should not be forced upon them. Although it is widely recognised that children need a *silent period*[2] during which they are introduced to language through a variety of practical and intellectual experiences, educators seem strangely reluctant to acknowledge that this fact also applies to the language classroom. Children will gain in confidence and motivation by studying English in an activity-based environment. They should be encouraged to work out for themselves what they want to say. They should be allowed to make mistakes without the fear of failure. In this way, a teacher is laying the foundations for a successful language learner. Have no doubt, children will speak in the classroom – and speak well – when they are ready to speak.

5. Errors and correction

The long term aim of teaching English is for the students to speak English confidently, correctly and fluently. However, it is neither reasonable nor desirable to have this expectation at the beginning of a language programme. Children may have ten or more years of language study ahead of them. In the early stages of a language course for children, it is important to establish priorities for the child as a learner. These include:

– building confidence;
– encouraging *ownership* of language. Children should *experience* English;
– teaching children to communicate with whatever language they have at their disposal (mime, gesture, key word, drawings, etc.);
– teaching children to treat language as a communication tool, not as an end product;
– showing children that English is fun;
– establishing a trusting relationship with the children, and encouraging them to do the same with their classmates;
– giving children an experience of a wide range of language in a non-threatening environment.

In addition, repeated correction of errors in the early stages of a language course fosters the following *negative* aspects:

– children lose confidence from fear of making mistakes;
– children only say what they know they can say;
– children become dependant on the teacher for correction;
– the need for language accuracy interferes with the need to communicate.

There are certainly times when children *do* want to know how to say something correctly, and there are times when correction may be necessary. Teachers should judge the importance of *errors* and *correction* with respect to the other factors that affect the success of learning for children. In all events, experience has shown that errors made in the early learning days do not become so ingrained that the children themselves cannot be guided to recognise them – when they have enough experience of the language to make such correction meaningful and productive.

6. The importance of group support

Speaking a foreign language requires the learner to take risks. To make mistakes in front of twelve others is a daunting experience for an eight-year-old child. Until children feel comfortable and secure in the class, they will learn very little. This sense of security takes time to develop. Lessons should incorporate many activities which encourage group support, fun and friendship. Furthermore, to make the most effective use of class time these activities can be adapted to fit in with the theme or language of the particular unit that is being studied.

7. Using their bodies

Children need to have the opportunity to use their hands and their bodies to express and experience language. In an everyday context in an English speaking country, children are quite naturally exposed to a variety of physical and intellectual experiences of language. In the foreign learning situation where children may have as little as one hour per week of English classes, it is vital to include physical activities where the focus is on the *physical response*, not speaking.[3]

The importance of providing physical and practical learning opportunities cannot be overstressed. For children, this type of input is a crucial step in the learning pathway. With respect to activity-based study, many of the preparation activities should incorporate physical response. This provides a foundation of active understanding of the English that will be needed for any given topic or project.

Course material, therefore, should encourage children to *do* a range of practical activities or tasks. These tasks will give *the language* a practical context that has obvious meaning to children. The results of the tasks – whether a chart, a badge, a beetle, or a collection of bottles – form a natural language text, created, and *owned* by the children themselves. The teacher can then go on to exploit and practise this language.

8. The age of the learner

An activity-based approach can be successfully used with children of all ages and nationalities. The activity content is chosen from activities which are common throughout the primary school years, and, if necessary, can be adapted to the country/culture of the children. Taking *measuring* as an example, six-year-olds may need much guidance in order to be able to use a ruler and standard units of measurement. On the other hand, ten-year-olds should be able to estimate measurements in advance, and measure extremely accurately with a variety of measuring tools. However, the task of *measuring* is relevant to both age ranges. The language that is generated from the activity is also relevant to both age ranges. The role of the teacher is to make sure the activity content is exploited to suit the developmental age of the children in the class, and, where necessary, to ensure that this content is adapted to the children's cultural experience.

9. The pace of a lesson

All children do not learn at the same pace. Pace is therefore a matter of experience, and sensitivity to individual needs. The temptation is often to work too fast through materials, rather than to exploit the ability and interest of the children. It is not necessary for all the children to complete all the activities. Moreover, when children have successfully mastered an activity, it is more useful to build on this success than to move on to the next unit.

It is also important to incorporate many changes of activity within one lesson. This means that the children should be introduced to language and content through a variety of short steps and activities. Some involve movement, others are more passive. Since the attention span of young learners can be extremely short, change of pace (and approach) within a teaching sequence is vital.

In terms of overall pace through a course, this very much depends on the teacher and the class. One of the strong features of activity-based materials is that learning is not tied to a linear sequence of structures and functions. Teachers are able merely to leave out that which they feel is too easy, too difficult, or not relevant to their particular class.

Finally, as the author of an activity-based course for children, I sincerely believe that if you enjoy teaching children, activity-based materials will give you the opportunity to teach them well.

Notes

1. The example and example tables are taken from *early bird 1, Teacher's Book 1* by David Vale (Cambridge: Cambridge University Press, 1990), and are reproduced by kind permission of Cambridge University Press.
2. Stephen Krashen is one of the writers who has discussed the concept of the silent period at some length, for example in *The Input Hypothesis: Issues and Implications* (London: Longman, 1985), where he points out the importance of the silent period in 'normal' second language learning by children coming to live in a foreign country. He notes that often insufficient account of this phenomenen is taken in formal language classes, where students are frequently expected to start speaking immediately (pp 9-12, 70).
3. James J. Asher is one of the researchers who has stressed the value of physical responses in his work on 'Total Physical Response' methods in language teaching. For further discussion on the effectiveness of this approach to language learning, see for example J.J. Asher *et al.*, 'Learning a second language through commands: A second field test', in J.W. Oller and P.A. Richard-Amato (eds), *Methods that Work* (Cambridge, Mass.: Newbury House Publishers, 1983), pp. 59-70.

The Role of Assessment by Teachers in School

Glenn Fulcher

1. Introduction

It has been common for students of English as a Foreign Language who wish to take some form of external examination to be tested in what may only be described as a 'formal' manner. This may involve simply reading and writing, as in the University of London (syllabus 161B) overseas paper, or in all skills including speaking, as in the University of Cambridge Local Examinations Syndicate First Certificate in English and Proficiency in English. In the latter case, oral ability is tested by the means of an oral interview. Indeed, from only a cursory glance at the range of proficiency tests in English as a Foreign Language (EFL) on the market, all testing methods are *examination-board* oriented, and not *school* oriented (See Alderson, Kranke and Stansfield, 1987).

What is meant by this? A school or institute in which students are following courses which lead to an external qualification may assess their own students in a number of ways, including formal testing, but *only* in order to place them in the appropriate class (Placement Testing) or to decide if they are making progress in their studies (Achievement Testing). In no case can the class teacher's assessment of the abilities of an individual student be recorded and used as part of the final grade in the external qualification.

This sharply contrasts with the situation in countries where the teacher's assessment of her own individual students does play a role in making up the grades on the final leaving certificate which is awarded. Even in the United Kingdom the Task Group on Assessment and Testing (1988) recommended assessment based in the school through the use of Standard Assessment Tasks in all subjects, whilst the introduction of the General Certificate of Secondary Education (GCSE) places great emphasis on course work and internal assessment, with the appropriate safeguards of moderation procedures. As a result of these developments, the University of Cambridge has introduced the International General Certificate of Education (IGCSE) which is aimed at overseas educational institutions. One of the syllabuses available is English as a Second Language (ESL), and this contains an element of coursework and internal assessment.

As coursework and teacher assessment of students is likely to become more widespread in the EFL world, it is the appropriate time to begin to ask questions about the nature of the assessment procedures used. Is assessment carried out by teachers *different* from the assessment in traditional examinations? That is, does it provide extra information to external examinations, does it overlap, or does it provide exactly the same information? If the latter turned out to be true, then there would be little justification for the expenditure of vast amounts of time, energy and money in training assessors and operating complex moderation systems. This is essentially a question of the *validity* of using teacher assessment, which would have practical consequences for the ways in which we choose to assess students.

No less important is the question of *reliability*. Are teachers capable of reliably assessing their own students? This essentially means following students' progress, using standard assessment tasks, and converting their observations into a number or a letter which represents the ability of any given student.

It was with these questions in mind that two studies were devised in order to analyse a number of assessment techniques. The studies were carried out in a particular context which may well be relevant to the findings, and indicate to the reader where these findings may be limited in terms of application to their own teaching situation. The English Institute in Cyprus has used the University of London GCE (syllabus 161B) overseas examination for many years as an 'end-product' examination for students after nine or ten years of study. With changes in teaching methodology and examinations within the United Kingdom it was decided that the IGCSE ESL examination may very well be appropriate for our use. In order to investigate how the internal and external assessment of students at this Institute were operating, all assessment techniques were analyzed in two studies, one during the academic year 1988/89, and one during 1989/90.

The first study was designed to answer the question of whether the internal assessment provided by the teachers provided insights into the ability of students which was not provided by any external examination. The second study was designed to confirm these findings and, further, to investigate the issue of the reliability of teacher assessment.

2.1. First study

During 1988/1989, 114 students studying at the English Institute received six assessments. Of these, four were externally marked examinations, one was an internally marked examination, and one was a simple letter grade representing the teachers' assessment of student abilities. These are summarised in Table 1.

Letter	Grade from	Code
A	University of Cambridge First Certificate in English	FCE
B	Internal Teacher Assessment of Abilities	TASS
C	English Language Testing Service: Grammar	GRAM
D	English Language Testing Service: Listening	LIST
E	Internal Mock GCE Examination	MOCK
F	University of London GCE English (Overseas 161B)	GCE

Table 1: Assessments used in the first study

The analysis of student results should provide a way in to the study of teacher-based assessment within the school. Of the assessment techniques listed in Table 1, it was hypothesised that B represented teacher-based assessment, with the possibility of E also having some relationship to the ways in which teachers grade internally. The internal teacher assessment of abilities (B) was carried out within the school at the end of the academic year, and took the form of a global mark on a scale of A to E with plus and minus points between the two extreme grades, thus giving 13 possible grade points. Teachers were asked to assign a grade on the basis of their impression of the achievement of each student throughout the school year in relationship to the syllabus which was being followed. As such, it represents a subjective and personal impression which was not controlled by any system of moderation or carefully constructed grade descriptors to aid the teachers in their task. The internal GCE Mock examination (E) was written and marked by teachers, although before marking papers a co-ordination meeting was held to ensure that work was being marked in a similar way by all members of staff. No teacher marked the work of a student whom he or she had taught during the year. The two English Language Testing Service Modules were pilot versions of the new International English Language Testing Service test (see Criper and Davies, 1988 and Hughes, Porter and Weir, 1988 for information on why changes were suggested, and The British Council Information, 1989, for the current format). However, the modules which have now come into service do not differ greatly from the pilot modules.

2.2. Analysis

As a first step in the investigation, all data from all measures were correlated (Table 2).

	FCE	TASS	GRAM	LIST	MOCK
TASS	.49				
GRAM	.68	.33			
LIST	.54	.36	.48		
MOCK	.69	.64	.63	.44	
GCE	.58	.34	.55	.29	.55

Table 2: Correlation matrix of assessments (Study 1)

The question posed was whether or not teacher assessment offers something which is valuable to the overall assessment which other measures do not tap. In order to explore this Principal Components Analysis (PCA) with Varimax rotation was used to further explore the correlation matrix.[1] The results are presented in Table 3.

	Factor 1	Factor 2	Factor 3
FCE	.658	.364	.461
TASS	.146	.946	.156
GRAM	.749	.120	.452
LIST	.160	.193	.928
MOCK	.574	.643	.262
GCE	.883	.187	-.002
Variance explained by rotated components (Eigen values)			
	2.149	1.529	1.371
Percent of total variance			
	35.825	25.476	22.848

Table 3: Rotating loadings on Factors from the PCA (Study 1)

It must be stressed that this study was exploratory. Principal Components Analysis has, in the past, been used in EFL studies in order to draw conclusions regarding the structure of language ability (Oller and Perkins, 1980), but many dangers lie in basing conclusions upon this type of analysis (Woods, 1983). One of the dangers will become clear in what follows.

It is the role of the investigator to label the factors which are produced from the analysis, primarily by using the measures which load highly on particular factors. It is then hoped that tentative hypotheses may be generated about the nature of assessment which may be followed up with a study using other techniques.

In this data, it may be observed that TASS loads very highly on Factor 2. This is followed by MOCK, which was the internally (teacher) assessed written examination. Factor 2 may therefore be labelled 'Teacher Assessment'. LIST loads most heavily on Factor 3, followed by FCE (which contains a listening and oral test), and GRAM. To label this factor we must assume that grammatical knowledge influences scores on aural/oral tests. This does not seem to be an unreasonable assumption. Factor 3 may therefore be called 'Aural/Oral Skills'.

GCE loads most highly on Factor 1, followed by GRAM, FCE and MOCK. The GCE examination primarily contains writing, reading and grammatical exercises; hence, we may assume, the unimportant loading on Factor 3. Grammatical accuracy would seem to be an important factor in the measurement, as indeed it is in the written components of the First Certificate examination. This factor may tentatively be called 'Writing/Reading/Grammatical skills'. This large category cannot be broken down further from this data, but the labelling may be supported by the fact that Factor 1 accounts for 35.82% of variance across measures, much higher than other factors.

In order to examine the relationship between the various measures on the factors isolated it is useful to use Factor Plots. Figures 1 to 3 show the relationship between measures on the three Factors generated by the analysis.

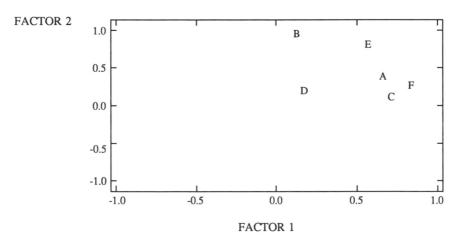

Figure 1: Factor plot for Factors 1 and 2 (Study 1).

FACTOR 3

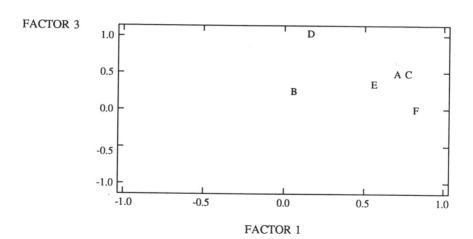

Figure 2: Factor plot for Factors 1 and 3 (Study 1).

FACTOR 3

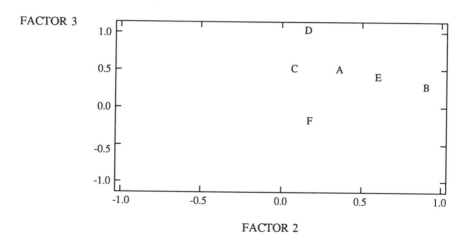

Figure 3: Factor plot for Factors 2 and 3 (Study 1).

2.3. Discussion

This type of exploratory analysis is, almost by definition, circular. For once factors are labelled, the labels are then used to interpret the loadings! However, placing this warning to one side, it does seem that teacher assessment (TASS)

143

is very different from other measures. It consistently stands alone on the Factor Plots.

The data suggest the hypothesis that teacher assessment is qualitatively different from other modes of assessment.[2] The only measure which loads on all three factors is FCE, which is a multi-skill examination, but recorded here as a global grade. It is also highly likely that the multi-skill ELTS examination taps all factors, but this is hidden here, as GRAM and LIST are reported separately, and the students in the sample did not sit the other components of the test.

15.85% of the variance in these measures was not accounted for in this analysis. It is possible that this is error variance, or may indicate the presence of other factors too small in their influence to be susceptible of analysis. No further explanation can be offered.

It may now be possible to begin to suggest an answer to the first of the questions posed through this exploratory analysis. Teacher assessment of students does seem to provide information not supplied by traditional written examinations, or aural/oral tests in language examinations. However, it would also appear equally true that teacher assessment alone cannot substitute for the information provided by these examinations.

It may be claimed that teachers are sensitive to aspects of student performance which should be assessed, but that this assessment should be balanced by external examinations with a broad skills base, such as the ELTS or the UCLES examinations, rather than a narrow skills base such as the GCE which is still used in many countries such as Cyprus. The IGCSE may therefore be considered as providing an alternative for overseas students at the age of 16. However, the results of the study do not tell us anything about how teachers assess students or whether their assessment is reliable.

With these tentative suggestions in hand from the first study, further questions remained: could the study be reproduced with a separate sample of students, and is teacher assessment a reliable measure of student abilities?

3. Second study

In the second study into the nature of teacher assessment 122 students were used, again from the English Institute, in the academic year 1989/90. However, some of the measures used in the study differed.

Once again, all students took a mock examination which was prepared and marked in exactly the same way as the previous year, the FCE and the GCE. Unfortunately, no ELTS grades were available, but changes were carried out in the way teachers assessed their students. This latter development allows further investigation into the nature of teacher assessment.

The single letter grade method which was employed prior to 1989/90 was a holistic approach which asked the teacher to give a global assessment of student abilities. The new system provided for componential grading in skill areas together with an assessment of the amount and quality of work produced by students outside class (homework). The components of assessment were: reading ability, writing ability, accuracy of spelling, grammatical accuracy and homework. Each component was to be graded on a Likert-type scale of 1 to 5, with 5 being very good and 1 being very poor. Listening and speaking ability were omitted due to the nature of the course which the students were following: these skills were not tested in the end-product examination. The measures used are summarised in Table 4.

Letter	Grade from	Code
A	University of London GCE (Overseas 161b)	GCE
B	Internal Mock GCE Examination	MOCK
C	Internally assessed Reading ability	READ
D	Internally assessed Writing ability	WRITE
E	Internally assessed Spelling ability	SPELL
F	Internally assessed knowledge of/ability in Grammar	GRAM
G	Internally assessed quality/quantity of homework	HOME
H	University of Cambridge First Certificate in English	FCE

Table 4: Assessments used in the second study

The issues to be investigated here are complex, and it was difficult to decide on the techniques which would shed most light on the questions which had been posed. Initially, although undoubtedly unsatisfactory in itself, it was decided to conduct another Principal Components Analysis on the data in order to discover if similar factor patterns emerged. This in itself, with a different sample, would at least tend to suggest whether or not the initial exploratory study was merely an artefact of the sample or not. Secondly, it was decided to regress the components of teacher assessment onto the GCE scores for the 122 students. On the basis of the results of the exploratory study it would be expected that the multiple correlation coefficient would not be exceptionally high, showing relative independence of teacher assessment from external examination results. These two techniques and the results are presented in Section 4.

With regard to reliability, two techniques were used. Firstly, each component of teacher assessment was treated as if it were a separate 'test item', providing a five item test. In this way it is possible to treat teacher assessment as a single test of 25 marks (5 for each component) and calculate Cronbach's alpha as a measure of internal consistency. Further, each item or component may be analysed separately in terms of reliability. This technique is preferable in this context to calculating inter-rater and intra-rater reliability, as the assessment is the judgement of the class teacher of a student's ability and work over a whole year. Reproducing exactly the same experience of each student with more than one teacher is not practically feasible, and hence the assessment given by more than one person potentially subject to invalidity. This would appear to be a strange argument for another reason: traditional approaches to reliability of judgement rely totally on the ability of two or more persons agreeing in their assessment (see Krzanowski and Woods, 1984), or correlating teacher assessments with some criterion test.[3] But with teacher assessment of her own students in the intimacy of the classroom over an extended period of time, it is suggested that the teacher possesses an understanding and depth of insight into the students' abilities which cannot be easily replicated.

Secondly, what little research has been done into the nature of teacher assessment has suggested that sources of unreliability stem from the effects of sex and age (Jasman, 1987). In the case of this sample all students were of the same age, and so this factor cannot be assumed to be a source of unreliability. However, it was decided to investigate the effect of sex through the use of Analysis of Variance. This allows the researcher to look at the potential effect of the sex of the student, the sex of the teacher, and any possible interaction effect between sex of the teacher and the sex of the student (do male teachers tend to favour boys or girls in assessment, and the same for female teachers). Of course, there are many variables which can affect scores (see Bachman, 1990:119 for examples), but it is often difficult to isolate all potentially confounding factors, let alone design a study which will take them into account. It is for the reader to judge whether or not other variables which have not been considered may be so important as to render this study of marginal value.

If, given the above assumptions, assessment is reliable, one would expect to see a high Cronbach alpha, reasonable item reliability statistics, and no effect of sex on scores. The investigation into reliability is presented in Section 5.

4.1. Principal Components Analysis

Once again, as a first step, Pearson correlation coefficients were calculated for all data (Table 5). From these figures attention should initially be drawn to the relationship between teacher assessment of writing and spelling with the external examination results on the GCE. This may lead us to think that certain aspects of teacher assessment do relate to formal examination results, but that other components tap other aspects of student ability, as suggested by the exploratory study.

146

	GCE	MOCK	READ	WRITE	SPELL	GRAM	HOME
MOCK	.71						
READ	.37	.44					
WRITE	.61	.77	.44				
SPELL	.61	.69	.38	.70			
GRAM	.49	.55	.24	.57	.60		
HOME	.42	.58	.23	.62	.54	.51	
FCE	.66	.64	.41	.57	.60	.43	.46

Table 5: Correlation matrix of assessments (Study 2)

Turning to the Principal Components Analysis, it was decided to retain a solution with three components. In the exploratory study three components were retained on the criterion that the Eigen value for each component should be greater than 1, but in this solution it was necessary to discover if the factor pattern was similar, even though listening was not assessed. It transpired, nevertheless, that the Eigen values associated with each component were indeed significant. Table 6 provides the results of the analysis.

	Factor 1	Factor 2	Factor 3
GCE	.285	.127	.854
MOCK	.555	.284	.632
READ	.119	.954	.222
WRITE	.675	.342	.463
SPELL	.615	.207	.544
GRAM	.763	.015	.292
HOME	.844	.091	.168
FCE	.250	.199	.821

Variance explained by rotated components (Eigen values)

	2.593	1.204	2.476

Percent of total variance explained

	32.414	15.045	30.947

Table 6: Rotating loadings on Factors from the PCA (Study 2)

McNemar (1951, quoted in Child, 1970:12) was among those who were highly critical of Factor Analysis and Principal Components Analysis, arguing with a large degree of fairness that 'when interpreting factors all factorists struggle and struggle and struggle in trying to fit the factors to their initial hypotheses.' Hence my initial comment that this approach to replication of results is not entirely satisfactory.

This caveat to one side, a fairly clear factor pattern does emerge from this study. Firstly, all formal examinations load more highly on Factor 3 than do any other forms of assessment. However, the teacher assessment of spelling and writing do load to some extent on this factor also, confirming the initial examination of the correlation matrix. The teacher assessment of reading loads highly on Factor 2 and on no other factors. An interpretation of this will be offered shortly. All forms of teacher assessment load most highly on Factor 1, followed by MOCK, which was internally assessed. No aural/oral factor emerged, but this is not surprising as the only component containing those elements was the FCE which, once again, was represented by a global grade including other skills.

This clear factor pattern removes some of the hesitation which the researcher may have in interpreting the results given the problems which exist in factor interpretation, and we may conclude that the results of the Principal Components Analysis do generally confirm the exploratory hypothesis that teacher assessment validly taps aspects of student abilities and performance to which external examinations are not sensitive, with the important rider that some aspects of teacher assessment do coincide with external examination results – in this case spelling and writing, as the GCE external examination does in fact place 70% of all marks on writing abilities.

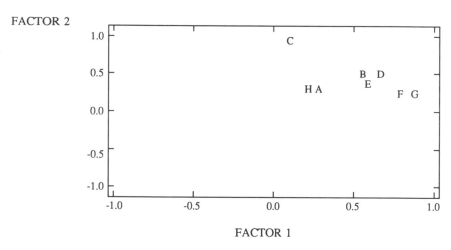

Figure 4: Factor plot for Factors 1 and 2 (Study 2).

Factor Plots are once again provided to allow the reader to conceptualise the relationships between measures on the three factors retained in the solution (Figures 4 - 6).

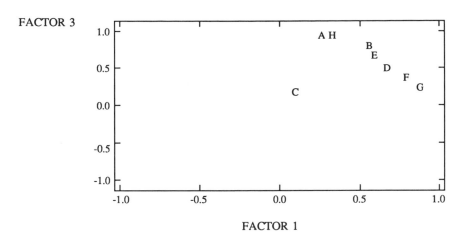

Figure 5: Factor plot for Factors 1 and 3 (Study 2).

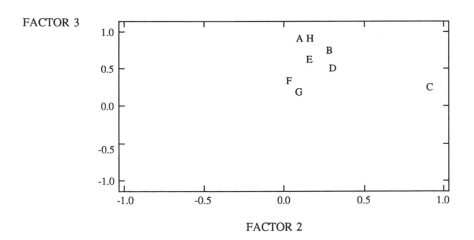

Figure 6: Factor plot for Factors 2 and 3 (Study 2).

4.2. Multiple regression

Each component of teacher assessment was regressed on the GCE score with the hypothesis that prediction from teacher assessment to external examination results would not be extremely high. The results of this part of the study are in fact extremely interesting, in that they confirm the conclusions drawn from the Principal Components Analysis. The results are presented in Table 7.

Variable	Coefficient	Std Error	Beta	Tolerance	T	P
READ	.182	.517	.112	.784	1.420	.093
WRITE	.419	.165	.278	.408	2.540	.012
SPELL	.432	.181	.244	.464	2.380	.019
GRAM	.200	.165	.112	.566	1.212	.228
HOME	.102	.128	.074	.537	.802	.424

N: 122   Multiple R: .660   Squared Multiple R: .435
Adjusted Squared Multiple R: .411   Standard Error of Estimate: 1.038

Table 7: Multiple regression of teacher assessment on GCE scores

It will be noted that although the multiple correlation coefficient is significant at .66 the variance shared with the external examination result is only .43, hardly large enough for accurate prediction of examination results. The adjusted squared multiple correlation is what may be expected in terms of prediction for any future sample of students drawn from the same population, and this is a lower .41. This tends to confirm the hypothesis, once again, that teacher assessment is offering something of value and validity in addition to the external examination results.

The final column in the table (P) provides the degree of significance of the correlation between the predictor and the examination results. Only writing and spelling are significant at $P < .05$, whilst the assessment of the amount and quality of work done outside the classroom is least significant in predicting results. We may be fairly confident of these findings as the Tolerance figures for all of the predictor variables do not approach zero, indicating that each of the independent variables is not so highly correlated with any other variable that we would suspect problems of collinearity: each of the variables does tap something unique as well as the variance it shares with other variables.

In 4.1 and 4.2 similar conclusions may be drawn, even though two separate techniques have been used. Teacher assessment of students does add something important to the overall assessment of students in addition to information provided by external examinations results.

5.1. Reliability

Teacher assessment may seem to be valid, but it cannot be valid if it is not reliable (Stevenson, 1981:47; Fulcher, 1987a:289; Bachman, 1990:160). Reliable assessment is a necessary but not sufficient condition for valid assessment. Each of the components of teacher assessment was treated as a single test item with a possible score of 1 to 5, with the total score possible on all items being 25. The reliability of teacher assessment as a global concept may then be assessed regarding reliability, and each component analyzed in terms of item reliability. The results of this investigation are presented in Tables 8 and 9.

Method of Calculation	Reliability Coefficient
Split-Half Correlation	.763
Spearman Brown Coefficient	.866
Guttman (Rulon) Coefficient	.846
Cronbach's Alpha Coefficient	.815

Table 8: Internal Consistency Data on Teacher Assessment as a single test

Label	Mean	Standard Deviation	Item-Total R	Reliability Index	Excluding this Item	
					R	ALPHA
READ	3.131	.829	.591	.490	.380	.840
WRITE	2.877	.829	.868	.774	.765	.726
SPELL	2.943	.761	.821	.624	.714	.749
GRAM	3.303	.756	.751	.568	.615	.777
HOME	3.336	.972	.770	.749	.591	.786

Table 9: Item Reliability Statistics,
with Teacher Assessment Categories treated as individual items

Cronbach's alpha for global teacher assessment is a very acceptable .815, surprisingly high in fact for the nature of the assessment process. Given their detailed knowledge of individual students, teachers do seem to be very consistent in the way they award grades.

In Table 9 we are primarily interested in the final column. This tells us what Cronbach's alpha would have been if this component of the assessment had been omitted. In each case, with the exception of the assessment of reading, the alpha coefficient would have been lower, indicating that total assessment would have been less reliable. Had the assessment of reading been omitted, however, coefficient alpha would have been a higher .84.

The assessment of reading ability by teachers (from those abilities investigated here) appears to be a problem area. This is confirmed by the correlation coefficient between this component and the total grade (.59) and the component reliability figure (.49). This may now be used to throw light on the fact that reading alone loaded on Factor 2 in the Principal Components Analysis. The assessment of reading stands alone because its assessment is essentially unstable. Why should this be so? Reading ability, unlike the other components, is an aspect of proficiency which cannot be directly observed. The classroom teacher may only *infer* the quality of reading ability by other means, such as the success with which the students handle comprehension exercises. It may be hypothesised that the same may be found with the assessment of listening ability. The teacher would need to be 'inside the head' of the student to be able to observe what is actually taking place in the reading process. It may be tentatively concluded that reading ability is best tested through a more formal reading test, while those aspects of ability which have more direct behavioral manifestations are reliably open to teacher assessment.

5.2. The effect of sex as potential bias in teacher assessment.

Using the sex of the student and the sex of the teacher as categorial variables, an Analysis of Variance was performed on each of the components of Teacher Assessment. The results were then analyzed for bias in assessment as a result of the sex of the student, the teacher, and any possible interaction effect. The results are presented in Tables 10 to 14. It is important to notice, when reading Tables 10 to 15, that the ERROR component is extremely large. Usually this is undesirable in an Analysis of Variance, but here it is both expected and desirable. As the Analysis of Variance is attempting to see how much variance is attributable to test bias (measurement error) the residual error is the amount of variance which is attributable to true score once the error stemming from sex bias is removed. A large residual error variance thus indicates that sex bias does not unduly influence measurement negatively.

Source	Sum of Squares	DF	Mean-Square	f-ratio	P
SEXS	.8391	1	.839	1.200	.276
SEXT	.005	1	.005	.008	.931
SEXS*SEXT	.005	1	.005	.008	.931
ERROR	82.566	118	.700		

Table 10: Analysis of Variance using READ as the dependent variable, and the sex of the teacher (SEXT) and sex of the student (SEXS) as categorial variables.

Source	Sum of Squares	DF	Mean-Square	f-ratio	P
SEXS	1.029	1	1.029	1.583	.211
SEXT	14.659	1	14.659	22.554	.000
SEXS*SEXT	0.127	1	.127	.195	.659
ERROR	76.694	118	.650		

Table 11: Analysis of Variance using WRITE as the dependent variable, and the sex of the teacher (SEXT) and sex of the student (SEXS) as categorial variables.

Source	Sum of Squares	DF	Mean-Square	f-ratio	P
SEXS	.224	1	.224	.390	.533
SEXT	2.115	1	2.115	3.690	.057
SEXS*SEXT	.003	1	.003	.005	.943
ERROR	67.630	118	.573		

Table 12: Analysis of Variance using SPELL as the dependent variable, and the sex of the teacher (SEXT) and sex of the student (SEXS) as categorial variables.

Source	Sum of Squares	DF	Mean-Square	f-ratio	P
SEXS	.292	1	.292	.565	.454
SEXT	6.065	1	6.065	11.730	.001
SEXS*SEXT	.167	1	.167	.323	.571
ERROR	61.012	118	.517		

Table 13: Analysis of Variance using GRAM as the dependent variable, and the sex of the teacher (SEXT) and sex of the student (SEXS) as categorial variables.

Source	Sum of Squares	DF	Mean-Square	f-ratio	P
SEXS	2.002	1	2.002	2.330	.130
SEXT	8.691	1	8.691	10.114	.002
SEXS*SEXT	.028	1	.028	.032	.858
ERROR	101.394	118	.859		

Table 14: Analysis of Variance using HOME as the dependent variable, and the sex of the teacher (SEXT) and sex of the student (SEXS) as categorial variables.

With the exception of reading, where there is no bias whatsoever, but which we have seen is an element of potential unreliability in assessment, the results are relatively easy to interpret. In no case does the sex of the student influence the teachers' assessments, nor is there any interaction effect between the sex of the student and the sex of the teacher. Thus, there is no evidence to suggest, for example, that male teachers treat female students preferably, nor is there any evidence to suggest any other combination of preferences which would constitute measurement error. However, in the cases of writing, grammar and homework there is an effect from the sex of the teacher. A post-hoc Tukey HSD test (not presented here as it is not of central relevance) confirms that male teachers awarded higher assessments than did female teachers in these areas.

In the case of writing this bias may only be apparent. As we have seen, the writing variable is the most accurate predictor of external examination results in the multiple regression. An Analysis of Variance using GCE results as the dependent variable and the sex of the teacher as the independent variable (Table 15) shows that the students of male teachers in this sample scored significantly higher than other students. As such, this apparent bias may merely be an artefact of this sample in which male teachers taught more proficient students and hence gave higher internal assessment grades to their students.

Source	Sum of Squares	DF	Mean-Square	f-ratio	P
SEXS	4.460	1	4.460	2.775	.098
SEXT	18.505	1	18.505	11.513	.001
SEXS*SEXT	2.118	1	2.118	1.361	.246
ERROR	189.666	118	1.607		

Table 15: Analysis of Variance using GCE as the dependent variable, and the sex of the teacher (SEXT) and sex of the student (SEXS) as categorial variables.

In the case of the assessment of the quality and quantity of homework the situation would seem to be much more clear cut. Male teachers are simply more lenient than female teachers.

6. Conclusions

From the two studies reported here, it would not seem unjust to conclude that teacher assessment within the school and classroom setting is valid in that it taps aspects of student abilities to which formal examinations are not sensitive. The experience the classroom teacher has of her students in the learning process should be taken into account. The classroom teacher can carry out the process of assessment reliably, although caution must be recommended in skill areas which are not more directly observable, as is the case with reading ability. Bias due to sex would not appear to be of any great concern at least as far as this sample is concerned.

The questions posed at the beginning of this article have been answered to some satisfactory degree for the specific situation to which they were relevant. The same questions will be relevant to other situations, but the population of teachers and students different. To the extent that they differ this kind of research must be carried out again to examine the issues of reliability and validity.

On the basis of this study, however, it would be recommended that EFL examinations should develop along the principle that externally set papers should be retained, but that continuous assessment by the teacher make up part of the final score or scores (if a profile reporting system is adopted) recorded on the certificate which the student receives. The UCLES IGCSE examination has begun this process by allowing some limited degree of internal teacher assessment. More experimentation along these lines would be beneficial in the interests of valid assessment.

This article has dealt exclusively with issues of reliability and validity. At the end of the day, however, practical considerations must be taken into account. And it is with these that we conclude. Achieving acceptable levels of reliability and validity in teacher assessment of students depends completely on each individual institution employing a fully professional and highly trained teaching staff. There are institutions in many countries which, given the opportunity of raising their students' grades, would jump at the chance in order to better sell the commercial product which they offer. Teacher assessment is not for them. The Examination Boards must be careful to vet thoroughly each application to run internal assessment schemes. Any mistake would open the abyss into which reliable and valid assessment would disappear. This cannot be emphasised too strongly. If safeguards against those who would exploit the system do not work, then the Examination Board itself would surely end up with a severely damaged reputation among respectable institutions, which could not easily be repaired. In everything which the Examination Boards do, they must observe the ethical rules of the profession as laid down in the *Standards for Educational and Psychological Testing* (American Psychological Association, 1985). Some consequences of not doing so are dealt with in Fulcher (1987b). Secondly, the institutions themselves must make resources available for in-service teacher training. Even with a highly professional staff this will increase levels of reliability. Thirdly, each institution operating internal assessment should have at least one member of staff who is a qualified measurement expert, capable of monitoring the assessment which takes place.

As for the teachers themselves, much groundwork needs to be covered. It needs to be ensured that the amount of extra work required in recording internal assessments does not place too high a burden upon them, given their normal teaching loads. If it does, it will be resented. Given the knowledge that 'their grades count' some teachers may be fearful of giving assessments which are too high or too low. These fears must be overcome in the interests of the students themselves. The management of change is important should a school decide that it wishes to operate internal assessment.

Teacher assessment will undoubtedly become an issue in the world of EFL teaching within the next ten years even though it is not furiously knocking on our door at the present time. The more EFL professionals can discover about it now the better placed we will be to cope with it when the need arises.

Notes

1. For readers unfamiliar with the statistical processes used in this article, and the issues regarding Factor Analysis in particular, see Woods (1983), and Woods, Fletcher and Hughes (1986). A very clear explanation of the conceptual background to the interpretation of Factor loadings may be found in Burroughs (1975:274-279), and a more wide ranging discussion is provided by Child (1970). For detailed information on all the techniques used in this study see the excellent work by Crocker and Algina (1986), and the classic work of Cronbach (1984). Henning (1987) also provides much useful background information. Simpler introductory material may be found in Hatch and Farhady (1982), Butler (1985), Isaach and Michael (1981), and Ferguson (1981). For language teachers with no background in measurement theory, introductory texts such as Hughes (1989) or Baker (1989) may be consulted. Selliger and Shohamy (1989) provide a very clear introduction to basic research techniques in the field of foreign language learning and assessment.
2. The problem with labelling Factor 2 'Teacher Assessment' in the exploratory study is that it is not a skill or ability (or constellation of skills or abilities) possessed by students, as are Factor 1 and Factor 3. This essentially means that whilst teacher assessment is different in kind from other measures, we are unable to say from the first study what teachers are taking into account when they assess. This problem is overcome in the design of the second study.
3. Recent research in the United States reported by Levine and Haus (1987) suggested that assessments of students made by teachers of French and Spanish differed significantly from their scores on standardised ratings of oral proficiency. The recommendations made in their study were that more rigorous teacher training should be introduced so that teacher assessments and standardised test results would coincide. Apart from any other consideration, if the two techniques provided the same information (their definition of reliability) then one technique would be redundant by definition. However, it should be noted that the results of the studies presented in this paper would suggest that the difference noticed by Levine and Haus may be important in its own right and not just the result of unreliable teacher assessment. Levine and Haus should, perhaps, begin to question the nature of that which they purport to be investigating rather than assuming that reliability and validity of teacher assessment can be judged solely on an external criterion using correlational studies.

Bibliography

Alderson, J.C., Krahnke, K.J. and Stansfield. 1987. *Reviews of English Language Proficiency Tests*. Washington, D.C.: Teachers of English to Speakers of Other Languages.

American Psychological Association. 1985. *Standards for Educational and Psychological Testing*. Washington, D.C.: APA.

Bachman, L.F. 1990. *Fundamental Considerations in Language Testing*. Oxford: Oxford University Press.

Baker, D. 1989. *Language Testing: A Critical Survey and Practical Guide*. London: Edward Arnold.

British Council. 1989. *Introduction to the IELTS*. London: The British Council.

Burroughs, G.E.R. 1975. *Design and Analysis in Educational Research*. University of Birmingham Faculty of Education: Educational Monograph No. 8.

Butler, C. 1985. *Statistics in Linguistics*. Oxford: Basil Blackwell.

Child, D. 1970. *The Essentials of Factor Analysis*. New York, etc.: Holt, Rinehart and Winston.

Criper, C. and Davies, A. 1988. *ELTS Validation Project Report*. The British Council/University of Cambridge Local Examinations Syndicate.

Crocker, L. and Algina, J. 1986. *Introduction to Classical and Modern Test Theory*. New York, etc.: Holt, Rinehart and Winston.

Cronbach, L.J. 1984. *Essentials of Psychological Testing*. New York: Harper and Row.

Ferguson, G.A. 1981. *Statistical Analysis in Psychology and Education*. Singapore: McGraw-Hill Book Company.

Fulcher, G. 1987a. 'Tests of oral performance: The need for data-based criteria', *English Language Teaching Journal* 41/4, pp. 287-291.

Fulcher, G. 1987b. 'Measurement or assessment: A fundamental dichotomy and its educational implications', *Education Today* 37/2, pp. 60-65.

Hatch, E. and Farhady, F. 1982. *Research Design and Statistics for Applied Linguistics*. Rowley, Mass: Newbury House.

Henning, G. 1987. *A Guide to Language Testing - Development - Evaluation - Research*. Rowley, Mass: Newbury House.

Hughes, A., Porter, D. and Weir, C. 1988. *Discussion on the ELTS Validation Report*. The British Council/University of Cambridge Local Examinations Syndicate.

Hughes, A. 1989. *Testing for Language Teachers*. Cambridge: Cambridge University Press.

Issac, S. and Michael, W. B. 1981. *Handbook in Research and Evaluation for Educational and the Behavioral Sciences*. San Diego, California: EdITS Publishers.

Jasman, M.A. 1987. *Teacher-based Assessments: A Study of Development, Validity and Reliability of Teachers' Assessments and Associated Structured Activities Devised to Assess Aspects of the Primary Curriculum for the Age Range 8 - 12 Years and the Evaluation of In-service Provision to Facilitate such Teacher-based Assessments*. University of Leicester: Unpublished Ph. D. thesis.

Krzanowski, W.K. and Woods, A.J. 1984. 'Statistical aspects of reliability in language testing', *Language Testing*, 1/1, pp. 1-20.

Leveine, M.G. and Haus, G.J. 1987. 'The accuracy of teacher judgement of the oral proficiency of high school foreign language students', *Foreign Language Annals*, 20/1, pp. 45-50.

McNemar, Q. 1951. 'The factors in factoring behaviour', *Psychometrica* 16, pp. 353-359.

Oller, J.W. and Perkins, K. 1980. *Research in Language Testing*. Rowley, Mass: Newbury House.

Selliger, H.W. and Shohamy, E. 1989. *Second Language Research Methods*. Oxford: Oxford University Press.

Stevenson, D.K. 1981. 'Beyond faith and face validity: the multitrait-multimethod matrix and the convergent and discriminant validity of oral proficiency tests', in Palmer, A.S., Groot, P.M.J. and Trosper, G.A. (eds), *The Construct Validation of Tests of Communicative Competence*. Washington, D.C.: Teachers of English to Speakers of Other Languages, pp. 37-61.

Woods, A. 1983. 'Principal components and factor analysis in the investigation of the structure of language proficiency', in Hughes, A. and Porter, D. (eds), *Current Developments in Language Testing*. London: Academic Press, pp. 43-52.

Woods, A., Fletcher, P. and Hughes, A. 1986. *Statistics in Language Studies*. Cambridge: Cambridge University Press.

Innovation and Development in English in Europe

Robert Wilkinson

1. Introduction

Over the past two years we have witnessed the most dramatic changes in Europe since the second world war. It was only in late November last year that a comprehensive peace settlement was signed in Paris at the Conference on Security and Cooperation in Europe. This somewhat neglected ceremony heralds perhaps an era of development and cooperation in Europe such as has never occurred before. Earlier eras of progress have been based on national competition, and, although we may point to the European Community as an example of cooperation between a limited number of states, it is equally possible to argue that the Community itself owes its existence to threats of competition both within Europe (for example between France and Germany, and between eastern and western Europe) and without (from the USA and more recently Japan and the Asian 'dragons').

Despite the fears expressed in some quarters of destabilization caused by the massive imbalance in wealth and productivity between eastern and western Europe, I would contend that the stage is set for unprecedented cooperation between communities such that the concept of the nation state may cease to be relevant. Much of the cooperation in Europe will be carried on through the medium of English, and as a result English will grow considerably and will necessarily be subject to change and development.

In economics it has long been recognized that the essential forces of growth are innovation and selection (Nelson and Winter, 1974) and it may be argued that the growth of languages is subject to the same forces. This article reflects on the background to innovation and selection in the growth of English in Europe before considering some of the likely areas of change and the consequent implications for English language learning and training in Europe.

2. Growth of English

Until recently, much research on language change in English has focused on the so-called mother-tongue varieties, that is those varieties spoken in what Kachru (1985) calls the Inner Circle: Britain, USA, Ireland, Australia, etc. There has also been considerable research into so-called second language varieties, functioning in Kachru's Outer Circle: India, Pakistan, parts of Africa, etc. Many investigators too have looked at features of English interlanguages in many countries of the Expanding Circle (e.g. Kachru, 1982; Quirk and Widdowson, 1985). However, few attempts have been made to examine systematically the influences that affect communication in English between speakers of other languages in the Expanding Circle, especially in situations where English mother tongue speakers may be absent. This is the kind of situation which will increasingly predominate in Europe as communities cooperate more across language boundaries.

English owes its success to the fact that it has always been a language amenable to change and innovation. This may well be due to the creole-like foundation of English, as a combination of various western Germanic languages, Norse, and Norman French, a foundation which has enabled English to absorb new words and modify syntax with considerable freedom. Yet amenability to change obviously cannot be seen as the sole source of success. In addition to evident factors in earlier centuries such as British maritime power and colonialism, factors in the twentieth century that play a role in this success include the economic, political, and military power of the USA, the extent of research in science and technology (especially in micro-electronics) conducted through English, mass tourism, transnational popular music, transnational television and advertising, publishers' market size, international scientific conferences, even the foreign-language policies of national education authorities. Even with these very powerful factors driving the expansion of English, it is unlikely that the language would have achieved such success without its innovative dynamism and flexibility.

3. Innovation

What drives innovation in languages? Before considering factors for change in English in Europe, it is worth looking at some more general forces driving innovation in languages. In this respect, economic forces may be more important than is often realized, as a cursory survey of innovative forces in industry may show.

The Schumpeter-Galbraith hypotheses indicate a positive relationship between innovation and monopoly power and that large firms are proportionately more innovative than small firms (Kamien and Schwartz, 1982). However,

160

neither hypothesis accounts for the driving forces of innovation. These may be seen as falling by and large into two groups: 'technology-push' innovation (Nelson, 1959; Phillips, 1966), where it is the underlying scientific knowledge that drives innovation, and 'demand-pull' innovation (Schmookler, 1966), where economic opportunity is the driving force. Transferring these ideas to innovation in English permits the contention that the vast vocabulary of English (its underlying scientific knowledge) is one of the driving forces impelling English to be used in new ways and new circumstances for new concepts and ideas: 'language supply-push' innovation. The necessary language is available, but it has not yet been employed in the particular circumstances. Secondly, the existence of a communication demand between speakers of other languages in order to reach a variety of instrumental goals also impels English to be used in innovative ways: 'language demand-pull' innovation. Here the language means for expressing particular concepts is not yet available, and so existing means are redefined to cover the new concepts or new means are invented or imported into the language, for example, from other languages.

The above analogy may indicate two different kinds of innovative force in language interaction, both functioning alongside each other. It may be that the latter type of force may represent much of the innovation occurring in the outer and extended circles. However, it is worth pursuing the economics analogy further with a view to looking at potential sources of innovation in Europe.

Schumpeter's hypothesis (1943) about the positive relationship between innovation and monopoly power entails, following Kamien and Schwartz's (1982) discussion, that a firm will be motivated to innovate if it can anticipate monopoly power, hence extraordinary profits. Equally, a firm already possessing a monopoly for some of its products is likely to be motivated to innovate, producing new products, in the hope of extending that monopoly. Such a firm may already have or be able to call upon the necessary resources (human and financial) to carry out the innovation because of its existing monopoly. However, not all monopoly firms are equally innovative: there are indeed ways in which possessing monopoly power may work to the disadvantage of innovation. A firm already realizing extraordinary profits on existing products may not wish to take the risk of reducing those profits or jeopardizing the monopoly on those products through the uncertainty of innovating; it may prefer to act conservatively, waiting until someone else innovates and then imitating. Thus, although possessing a monopoly is helpful for innovation, the firm most likely to innovate may not possess full monopoly power. Consequently the structure of market in which the firm is operating in is crucial: innovation appears to be related to the 'intensity of rivalry' in the market (Kamien and Schwartz, 1982; van Witteloostuijn, 1990), and a market in which there are a small number of potential innovators seems to be the most prospicious for innovation.

Although at present this argument may appear to be of only marginal relevance to innovation in English in Europe, it may prove useful to consider briefly van Witteloostuijn's (1990) discussion of competition in multimarket scenarios with a view to applying the hypothesis to the role of English in Europe, before returning to the importance of innovation in the language.

Competition in multimarkets is defined by van Witteloostuijn as 'rivalry among competitors which operate in a set of related markets' (1990:237). Related markets may be upstream (e.g. raw materials suppliers) or downstream (e.g. consumer markets) in the production chain or sideways (e.g. related products markets) or geographically dispersed. A firm operating in a multimarket scenario may adopt a policy to integrate the upstream or downstream businesses or a policy to diversify horizontally into related markets. When firms in related markets attempt or threaten to move into each other's markets, or indeed only offer the potential threat of doing so, then multimarket competition comes fully into play, with corollary spillover effects: changes in the activities of one firm in one market may influence the strategies adopted by another in a second market which in turn may affect the activities of the first.

Let us treat Europe as a multimarket situation with a large number of competing languages and cultures. No single language holds monopoly power. English may be the dominant language, but it does not have a monopoly: German is fast becoming the challenger. There is certainly no monopoly culture (assuming we exclude for the purposes of this argument transnational trends like fast-food outlets!). Languages are indeed in competition with each other, despite the best intentions of the European Community not to favour any one national language at the expense of the others. It is this kind of situation where innovation is at its greatest: the competition is relatively intense, and there is not a total monopoly. Indeed, if there were a monopoly, (i.e. where English might be the monopoly language), and this monopoly were accepted, then following the economic argument less innovative change would be likely. Some competitors too may find the intensity of rivalry a little too intense and decide to cut their losses and pull out: would it be stretching the analogy too far to say that this is what has happened to French since the 1960s?

4. Selection

Throughout its history English has been constantly subject to new developments, as new ideas, concepts, objects, situations have come to be expressed in English. Just as in the natural world, the language is subject to evolutionary processes as certain expressions become outdated and consequently eliminated from contemporary usage and others are adapted to suit new circumstances. Although one should perhaps not pursue the Darwinistic analogy too far, there will be few observers who dispute an evolutionary process in language change. One could argue that the concept of the survival of the fittest is equally applicable to language growth in that those expressions that are most productive have a greater chance of survival.

This leads on to the relative efficiency of language expressions. There are two sides to efficiency, directing what is available to its most productive use, and producing a given amount from a minimum of resources. From the point of view of learners, it is easy to understand how languages may be used efficiently in either sense, especially where informative and transactional language are concerned. These efficiency 'rules' would inevitably lead to least-efficient expressions being 'selected out' over time. Thus, in a European context where communication between speakers of different languages increasingly takes place through the medium of English, the speakers are likely to use more frequently those expressions that prove communicatively efficient. Correspondingly the other two great E's, effectiveness and economy, also play important roles in international communication. (This would seemingly accord with Grice's (1975) cooperative principle.) On the other hand, in communication in English between speakers of other languages (for example, business or commercial discussions), we may observe considerable repetition, often where one party to the discussion repeats or rephrases what another party has uttered.[1] This would appear to flout both the efficiency and the economy of communication. Moreover, English native speakers may occasionally experience irritation at what they see as an unnecessary prolongation to a discussion, and yet it is pertinent to ask whether English monocultural discussions are any more efficient, with all their irrelevant asides, etc. Nevertheless, the increase in international communication in English would seem to lead inevitably to greater efficiency.

Evolutionary selectivity brings forth the concept of 'survival value'. This is not concerned with the language taught on so-called 'Survival English' courses, designed to help learners acquire enough of the language so that they can 'survive' in an English-speaking country. Rather, this is concerned with the value that any expression may have in terms of the likelihood of its continuing to be of use in the future. In this paper the concept is being used in relation to the actual or potential innovations in the variety of English used in Europe (excluding the native speaker areas). Such innovations may include new words to express new ideas (for example, the many new words produced by international organizations such as the EC) or new idiomatic expressions which may be coined by translating idioms from other languages into English. In the latter case a new idiom may have a high survival value if it also occurs in, say, three languages (e.g. German, French and Italian).

The discussion here may be concluded by reiterating a hypothesis that the growth of English in the new era of cooperation in Europe will be a factor of its intensity of innovation and the degree of selectivity. However, these cannot be seen as the only factors influencing growth. Other factors existing both at a community level and at an individual level would contribute to the development of a variety of English in Europe.

5. Developmental factors

The first group of developmental factors are those at a community level and include factors such as the role and activities in other language groups in Europe and the degree of intercommunication between them. This is closely linked to the activities in non-European language groups, especially perhaps Japan and the Asian 'dragons'. Inward investment on a pan-European scale is likely to be largely through the medium of English. Also within this group of factors comes of course the single market programme of the EC, which too will exert a heavy influence on the development of English. Activities too such as the current attempts by the European Federation of Stock Markets to create a unified European Stock Market, likely to be coordinated from Brussels, will also be contributing factors.

The second group comprises those at an individual or personal level such as communication needs, cultural differences, and identity (Wilkinson, 1989, 1990). The first refers to the language needs as perceived by the learner, which differ widely from those perceived by the school, company, education authority, etc. Learners may well have little incentive or motivation to continue learning when they feel they have satisfied their communication needs. The second covers the cultural differences that exist between different societies. As research has shown (Hofstede 1980, 1983), not only do different cultures hold very different values, but these cultural values are very deep-seated and almost immutable. People do not change their values very easily at all: they will rather carry over their own national values into the foreign language, and in line with the aim of many training courses, the best one can hope for at an aggregate level is that people achieve a heightened awareness of cultural differences. The third category to be mentioned here is identity: acquiring full native speaker equivalent competence in English would be tantamount to the acquisition of a new identity. Most learners, even the very successful ones, have little desire to reject, even partially, their own native identity; many naturally would prefer to add the new language culture to what they are already and so enhance their identity. A number of studies surveyed by Zuengler (1989) have shown that shared identity characteristics such as ethnicity, occupation, education, or gender may influence language learners' language away from, or perhaps towards, the standard language norm. Similarly, the degree of relative 'expertise' in the field under discussion can also influence language ability away from standard norms.

These two groups of factors, together with the forces of innovation, will have considerable influence on the future development of English in Europe. It is interesting to speculate on the areas of potential change and consider the issues that arise for teaching English in Europe.

6. Potential change

Studies reported elsewhere (Wilkinson, 1990) suggest that the areas of potential change in English in Europe are likely to concentrate on certain low level grammatical changes. These may include a gradual decline of mass/count distinction with expressions like 'much activities', 'less cars' becoming acceptable, and certain morphological changes such as the decline of the '-er', '-est' inflections in adjectives ('more clear', 'most bright'). Both of these features, however, seem to reflect a tendency apparent for quite some time in both British and American English. Similarly, certain changes in conditional clause forms may become acceptable, with the modals 'will' and 'would' being used in the condition, ('If more firms would adopt the system, exchange of information across Europe would be swifter'). It is noteworthy that this too is a feature of certain varieties of American English (see Kellerman, 1984).

Another candidate area for change is the use of the existential 'there'. It is possible that the range of structures permitted after 'there' could be extended to include passives. For example, 'there is mentioned a number of interesting ideas which deserve further investigation'. This is an area which does not seem to mirror a native speaker variety.

There may also be many changes in the areas of meaning. One likely area of change is in the use of clausal and sentential connectives, where words like 'next to', 'apart from', 'besides', etc., may acquire a range of meanings that differ somewhat from those they hold in inner circle varieties. Similarly, intersentential connectives such as 'however' or 'therefore' may extend their syntactic environments and indicate a relationship holding between subordinate and main clause, in much the same way as 'otherwise' and 'so' seem to. This, though, may not differ from a tendency in the inner circle.

A further likely area of change could be in certain verbal group meanings. For example, the scope of the use of the present perfect may change, particularly in view of the noted difficulty learners have in acquiring inner circle norms. One cannot neglect the differences in usage within the inner circle varieties either ('Have you eaten yet?' 'Did you eat yet?'). The range of meanings carried by modal verbs may well be subject to change, though one might argue that the modal verb system has always been a rather fluid area since the meaning carried by the modal is attitudinal and therefore is highly dependant on the individual speaker/writer (compare the important interaction between intonation pattern and modal verb).

Perhaps a slightly longer term field of change could be the prepositional system. Since prepositional systems in languages seem to be highly idiosyncratic, and since it is a area where learners of English typically experience difficulty, it is likely that subtle changes could be expected to arise gradually here.

The potential changes cited so far tend to be based on areas of language where European learners of English characteristically produce 'deviant' forms or expressions in relation to the inner circle norms. (One cannot ignore the fact that inner circle norms cannot always be expressed in precise terms, so that 'deviance' from one inner circle variety may not be 'deviance' from another.) Although I am considering these areas in terms of a dynamic 'development', by looking at them statically it is possible to see them as examples of language 'fossilization' in that the learners have no incentive to 'improve' once satisfactory communication is achieved. Few would doubt that effective communication can be achieved in a 'deviant', less 'elaborate' variety providing all parties to the communication adhere to or share similar 'conventions'. The majority of users of English in Europe may well be non-native speakers (although it is becoming increasingly difficult to say who is and who is not a native speaker), and the recognition of so-called 'deviant' forms as acceptable (and efficient) means of communication will necessarily depend on the extent to which these forms are shared across different language communities: in time 'deviance' may no longer be 'deviance', but standard. Its sharedness, however, can hardly be termed innovation, though there may be some innovative aspects to it.

Where innovation is likely to play a major role in the development of a European variety of English is in the area of lexical change. The European institutions, already referred to above, and other transnational associations and groupings will be a significant influence in the generation of new words and expressions to denote new or altered concepts in the rapidly changing European arena. Multinational enterprises which adopt a policy of using English in their internal communications will naturally have a considerable impact on the English of their personnel and subsequently their families. (The influence is of course both top-down and bottom-up, for the personnel of a firm will have much influence on the kind of English used in the firm.) What could be an even more important arena for language innovation is the low ground of ordinary person-to-person contact, where language is at its most dynamic because of the fluidity and relative informality of the contact, (as exemplified in the BBC series *The Story of English*). Such contacts could increase the demand for a greater tolerance of ambiguity (both referential and lexical), at least in the early stages of development.

It will be clear from the above discussion that the kind of English functioning internationally across Europe will be largely pragmatic and instrumental; it will include little of the cultural dimensions of inner circle varieties. To a great extent this pragmatic lingua franca will evolve other ways of categorizing reality (Hofstede, 1986), in the same way that the world seen through Indian English differs from that seen through British English. It will, however, be a vehicle for the partial transmission and interchange of the cultural values of the different European communities. European cultural diversity in itself will impel the 'indigenization' of this pragmatic English (Richards, 1978) and its evolution into a distinct variety as a result of its widespread use in new social and cultural contexts.

7. Implications for EFL in Europe

There are a number of questions which arise in connection with EFL in Europe, such as the extent to which teachers need to be aware of changes in current usage in English in Europe and the extent to which they should encourage such an awareness in their learners. This would naturally depend on who the learners are: schoolchildren, prospective English teachers, business people, etc., all have different requirements. It may be that schoolchildren ought to be introduced to British or American culture: prospective English teachers certainly are. What is, however, an increasing trend in many Business English courses is the tendency to confront learners with multiculturality and to foster an awareness of cultural differences through the medium of English.

In learner-directed learning, where the activities often involve some kind of 'fuzzy' problem-solving (as in simulations) and where information asymmetries permit opportunities for innovative language use, the trainer will have to consider the degree of intervention necessary, if at all, in an attempt to achieve a balance between communicative efficiency and language accuracy. This is likely to increase the difficulty teachers have in deciding on questions of norms and standards. (It may possible in time for ELT organizations throughout Europe to agree on standards and norms for the pragmatic variety of English, perhaps following on the lines of the threshold level (van Ek, 1977).)

A further question will arise with the development of 'European' idioms and metaphors and changes of meaning where European connotations of particular words differ from inner circle connotations (e.g. 'interesting', 'eventual', 'actual', 'realize', 'problem'). It is likely too that certain idiomatic usage will be understood in limited geographical areas: it is a moot point as to how much idiom is transferable across the Germanic-Romance linguistic boundary – perhaps more than one might think.

These issues also give rise to discussion of a number of areas of training where research is required. For example, research needs to be conducted into the value of sending language trainees for placement in countries or regions whose mother tongue they are unfamiliar with and where English is likely to be the main language of communication. The evolution of meaning changes in Europe and the process of recognition and avoidance of idiom/metaphor need to be investigated. Research too is needed into the production of ELT materials in Europe, into the effectiveness of transfer from one linguistic community to another. This of course cannot be studied independently from investigations into levels of acceptability and appropriacy, especially in relation to the power of the intended audience. Similar research could be undertaken to unearth common ground in international business and commercial communication.

8. Conclusion

In this article I advanced the argument that the forces of innovation and selection apply to the growth of English in Europe, inasmuch as they do to the growth of industry. (One should bear in mind all the reservations that apply to analogies, in particular that only certain features bear similarities.) Although acting on a different plane, the economic forces are interacting with other factors at both the community and the individual levels to foment a period of dynamic growth in a pragmatic variety of English in Europe such as the continent has not seen since the spread of Latin. This implies considerable challenges for English language teaching in Europe which need urgent consideration but which should be addressed with care.

Note

1. This has been a noticeable feature of discussions I have observed between groups in the Euregion (comprising the border regions of Aachen in Germany, Dutch Limburg, and the Belgian provinces of Limburg and Liège) where discussions between the speakers of German, French and Dutch usually take place in English (interpreters are not used). Tim Sebbage has reported the same feature (personal communication).

Bibliography

Grice, H.P. 1975. 'Logic and conversation', in Cole, P. and Morgan, J. (eds.), *Syntax and Semantics 3: Speech Acts*. New York: Academic Press.

Hofstede, Geert. 1980. *Culture's Consequences: International Differences in Work-related Values*. Beverly Hills: Sage.

Hofstede, Geert. 1983. 'Dimensions of national cultures in fifty countries and three regions', in Deregowski, J.B., Dziurawiec, S. and Annis, R.C. (eds.), *Expiscations in Cross-Cultural Psychology*. Lisse NL: Swets and Zeitlinger.

Hofstede, Geert. 1986. 'Cultural differences in teaching and learning', *International Journal of Intercultural Relations* 10, pp. 301-320.

Kachru, Braj B. (ed.). 1982. *The Other Tongue. English Across Cultures*. Urbana-Champaign: University of Illinois Press/Oxford: Pergamon Press (1983).

Kachru, Braj B. 1985. 'Standards, codification and sociolinguistic realism: The English language in the Outer Circle', in Quirk and Widdowson (1985).

Kamien, M.I. and Schwartz, N.L. 1982. *Market Structure and Innovation*. Cambridge: Cambridge University Press.

Kellerman, Eric. 1984. 'The empirical evidence for the influence of the L_1 in interlanguage', in Davies, A., Criper, C. and Howatt, A.P.R. (eds), *Interlanguage*. Edinburgh: Edinburgh University Press.

Nelson, R.R. 1959. 'The simple economics of basic scientific research', *Journal of Political Economy* 67.

Nelson, R.R. and Winter, S.G. 1974. 'Neo-classical vs. evolutionary theories of economic growth: critique and prospectus', *Economic Journal* 84.

Phillips, A. 1966. 'Patents, potential competition, and technical progress', *American Economic Review* 56.

Quirk, R. and Widdowson, H.G. (eds.). 1985. *English in the World*. Cambridge: Cambridge University Press.

Richards, Jack C. 1978. 'Models of language use and language learning', in Richards, J.C. (ed.), *Understanding Second and Foreign Language Acquisition*. Rowley, Mass.: Newbury House.

Schmookler, J. 1966. *Invention and Economic Growth*. Cambridge, Mass.: Harvard University Press.

Schumpeter, J.A. 1943. *Capitalism, Socialism and Democracy*. London: George Allen and Unwin.

van Ek, J.A. 1977. *The Threshold Level for Modern Language Learning in Schools*. Harlow: Longman.

van Witteloostuijn, Arjen. 1990. *Rationality, Competition and Evolution: Entry (Deterrence) in Dynamic Barrier Market Theory*. Maastricht: University of Limburg.

Wilkinson, Robert. 1989. 'Trends in European English', in Niemann, G. and Lee, A. (eds.), *Protokoll der fünften Tagung der Arbietsgruppe 'Fremdsprachen' der Bundesarbeits-gemeinschaft 'Gemeinsame Studienprogramme'*. Oestrich-Winkel: European Business School.

Wilkinson, Robert. 1990. 'Translating into European English: evolution and acceptability', in Thelen, M. and Lewandowska-Tomaszczyk, B. (eds.), *Translation and Meaning, Part 1*. Maastricht: Euroterm.

Zuengler, J. 1989. 'Identity and L_1 development and use', *Applied Linguistics* 10/1.

Theory and Practice in Language Teaching

Tim Caudery

1. Views on Theory

A colleague whose teaching I admire greatly once told me that she was not interested in following a Royal Society of Arts Diploma course in Teaching English as a Foreign Language because she thought it would be 'too theoretical, and not relevant to my teaching'. As the audience left the hall after a talk given by David Nunan at the 1991 conference of the International Association of Teachers of English as a Foreign Language I overheard one person say to another: 'That was too academic for me, I didn't find it relevant.' The talk had been on research into the reasons teachers gave for deviating from their lesson plans. A colleague described TESOL conferences disparagingly to me as 're-searchers giving papers and teachers listening'. McDonough and McDonough (1990) observe that 'teachers do not always perceive the findings of research as relevant to their classrooms and their own teaching practices. It is not even particularly unusual to find "theory" rejected outright, with a preference being stated for "practical hints", "new ideas", or "more techniques", that can be used directly in the classroom'. It would seem that there is quite a commonly held view, at least among teachers, that researchers/academics/theoreticians produce ideas which they expect to feed 'downward' to teachers operating in the language classroom, and, further, that such ideas are often irrelevant to actual teaching.

If by 'theory' we understand 'conclusions based on academic research', then it is certainly true that there are specific instances of poor quality research in the fields of language learning/teaching (as is likely to be the case in any academic field), and also of research which does not seem immediately applic-able to the classroom. Indeed, there may be great danger in placing too much reliance on academic research and applying its apparent findings uncritically to the classroom, as Noam Chomsky (1966; quoted in Allen and Corder, 1973: 212) was at pains to point out:

> I am, frankly, rather sceptical about the significance, for the teaching of languages, of such insights and understandings as have been attained in linguistics and psychology. ... [I]t is difficult to believe that either linguistics or psychology has achieved a level of

theoretical understanding that might enable it to support a 'technology' of language teaching. .... [S]uggestions from the 'fundamental disciplines' should be viewed with caution and scepticism.

Though much progress has been made since that was written, Chomsky's warning cannot yet be disregarded.

No doubt, too, there have been theoreticians who have been guilty of demonstrating an arrogant attitude concerning the application of their ideas in other people's teaching. Yet these points would not seem to justify the sweeping rejection of all 'theory' in any field. A degree of caution and scepticism among practitioners when evaluating new ideas would seem healthy and normal; to find significant numbers of practitioners ignoring new thinking, automatically dismissing it as irrelevant, would not. Why, then, are so many EFL teachers dismissive of 'theory'? Are such teachers simply wrong – obtuse, obstinate, ostrich-like – or is there something about TEFL as a field which makes it different from many others, at least as far as the relationship between theory and practice is concerned?

Typically, in practical projects, one would expect theory to inform practice. The bridge-builder uses his/her knowledge of civil engineering theory to design a bridge which is not identical to any other that has been built before, confident even at the design stage that when the first train rumbles over the completed structure, it will not collapse in a pile of rubble. Theories can of course be wrong; the coach who uses modern football theory to devise a new tactical approach for his team cannot be sure that it will defeat the opposition – but still the plan decides what the team will try to do, theory informs practice. Is this not the case in TEFL?

One surface indicator that there is indeed something unusual about TEFL in respect of the theory/practice relationship is the fact that the topic has been viewed by so many as meriting considerable discussion. H.H. Stern, for example, conducts an extended discussion of the role of theory in the field in the early chapters of his *Fundamental Concepts of Language Teaching* (Stern, 1983:23-72); in this discussion, he cites other views on the subject by, among others, Brown (1980), Spolsky (1978 and 1980) and Ingram (1980). McLaughlin (1987:1-18) discusses the nature of language learning theory at some length. Many other instances of discussions of the topic could be cited. One fashionable distinction to make nowadays in such discussions is between 'teacher initiated research' and 'academic research' – often with the implication that the first is superior to the second.

It is also possible to suggest plausible reasons as to why TEFL should be different in its use of theory from other practical applications, at least in some respects. One is that TEFL draws on many other disciplines for its theoretical base, and it may be debatable indeed which theory is relevant and which is not. Another is that some of these disciplines are relatively young fields of study. Ellis's claim (1983:283) that '[Second Language Acquisition] research is scarcely more than fifteen years old' might be disputed, but language learning and language teaching go back thousands of years – so there is certainly a tradition of language teaching to draw on which relies as much on trial and error, and craft knowledge passed on from one teacher to another, as it does on academic research. As far as language teaching theory is concerned, there are indeed plenty of theorisers putting forward ideas intended to inform teaching practice – but the ideas of different theorists frequently seem to contradict each other, asserting diametrically opposite points of view on occasion. Fashions come and go: overt grammar teaching is in vogue, then out, then in again; teaching using students' L_1 is normal in one decade, totally unacceptable the next, back again in modified form in a third. Yet despite these shifts in teaching style – for some teachers at least have always put into practice what the theorists advocated – learners have continued to learn foreign languages with a degree of success. This is perhaps not a fact which inspires confidence in the ability of teaching theorists to inform teaching practice; and it leads to a further important point: how can theory inform practice when it cannot adequately explain it? The civil engineer can explain exactly how and why the railway bridge does not collapse, but no-one can yet fully explain how language is learned in any context, and in particular how it is learned in the classroom. McLaughlin (1987:58) describes second language learning as 'a field where there are so many unresolved theoretical and practical issues and where so many research questions remain unanswered'. As Freeman puts it, '[t]he outcome [of language learning] is clear, but the process is not' (1989:28). If nevertheless language learning does go on in language classrooms, then perhaps there really is some evidence to suggest that the practitioners do not need the theorists.

So how *do* teachers of EFL make use of 'theory' – if they make use of it at all? Does it actually matter whether or how they use theory? And if it does, what implications does this have? These are questions which will be discussed in this paper.

2. Some definitions

2.1. Practitioners

For the purposes of this article, I will define the 'practitioners' of TEFL as the teachers involved in teaching particular courses. I regard them as practitioners both when they are planning their teaching and when they are carrying it out. Their planning may involve writing or modifying teaching material; it could therefore be argued that writers of published teaching materials should also be defined as 'practitioners', but I am here interested in the teachers who have the final say on what teaching goes on in the classroom – who actually decide teaching practice. Even when they 'follow' a published course, they are usually free to adapt the teaching material. Writers of published teaching materials are not writing for a particular learner or group of learners, and, while they may influence practice to a great degree, they do not have the final say.[1]

2.2. Theory

Finding a satisfactory definition of language teaching theory is surprisingly fraught with difficulties. Indeed, at least some of the differences in view on the role of theory in language teaching result purely from differences in definition. Some of the teachers I quoted in the opening paragraph of the article seem to be defining 'theory' as 'that which is not relevant to practice'; clearly, if we accept such a definition, further debate on the theory/practice relationship is a waste of time! Stern, on the other hand, finds that he can only define language teaching theory in very broad terms, as 'the thought underlying language teaching' (1983:23). This definition again renders non-existent any possibility of a discussion of *whether* theory relates to practice. However, it does not preclude discussion of *how* theory is related to practice. Furthermore, it makes practice the starting point in exploring the theory-practice relationship. This is a useful approach for this paper, since I am especially concerned with the way in which practitioners make use of theory.

In fact, it is difficult not to make one's definition of 'theory' a broad one, since any definition which is more precise excludes categories of thought which could be described in certain circumstances as 'theory'. I shall therefore use Stern's definition as a starting point, noting, however, that 'thought' is a rather vague term to use in a definition, and taking it to refer to ideas and principles more than to the active process of thinking something out.

Language teaching theory thus defined can clearly include many different categories. For example, we are concerned with both the teacher's own thought (ideas) and the thoughts of others which may be used by the teacher. The categories of theory used in teaching will be different for different teachers, but some theory categories which might underlie teaching practice are shown in Figure 1.

Published 'scientific theory' based on academic research	Published methodological theory of language teaching	'Craft knowledge' derived from training and/or experience	Personal beliefs, prejudices, principles	'Case theory' (ideas formed about current teaching task)

Figure 1. Categories of theory

Obviously this is not intended to be an exclusive list of types of theory. In this representation, the categories are not 'ranked'; in this respect, the figure differs from other models of language teaching theory, for example Stern's (1983:44). Where there is conflict between ideas in different categories, the individual will decide in each case which theory to give preference; it will not necessarily be the theory which is best supported by 'scientific' data, but simply the theory on which the practitioner decides to rely most, for whatever reason.

These categories of theory are far from being discrete. Each will be shaped by the others. For example, personal beliefs may be affected by published theories of others; and interpretation of the published theories of others may be affected by personal beliefs.

It would be possible for an individual's body of teaching theory to be entirely the result of his or her own thought; but it would be an enormous waste of time if every language teacher reinvented all the techniques of language teaching, and in practice of course most of our teaching theory is obtained from other people. However, in any individual the ideas of others may be partially known, distorted, misunderstood, or reinterpreted. In the final analysis, all the 'thought' underlying teaching practice is mediated by the teacher's own thinking.

The categorisation above separates theory mainly according to origin. One could also categorise language teaching theory in terms of subject area, since theory in a variety of disciplines might be considered relevant to language teaching. Theories of language acquisition (for both L_1 and L_2) are obviously very important, and themselves draw on a variety of areas of study. But I would suggest that the area of language teaching is even wider than that of language learning; psychology, sociology, general pedagogy, linguistics, and other fields are all relevant in various ways to the process of teaching languages. For fuller discussion of this issue, see for example Stern (1983) and, on a rather smaller scale, Freeman (1989). Stern (p. 47) describes his discussion of 'what different disciplines contribute to pedagogy' as 'the main theme' of his book; Freeman argues that the role which should be played by theory of education has long been underestimated in training language teachers.

2.3. Theorists

The definition I have adopted means that anyone whose 'thought' is used, directly or indirectly, in language teaching practice is a language teaching theorist. This category includes the thinker who proposes explanations to fit known facts, the researcher who seeks evidence to support a hypothesis, the scientist whose research was not conceived with language teaching in mind but which others have perceived as relevant, the language teaching materials writer who publishes materials that have been tried out in the classroom and found to 'work' (and also the materials writer who publishes materials that have not been properly trialled!), and – significantly – teachers themselves.

3. Theory used in teaching

As noted above, theory will be applied at two stages of the teaching process – in the planning stage, and in the actual teaching in the classroom. In the talk at the IATEFL conference mentioned earlier, David Nunan described research work in progress on the thinking behind *ad hoc* decisions made during teaching (Nunan, 1991). However, it is in the planning stage that most lessons are shaped, and perhaps there that we can as teachers be most easily aware of the thinking – theory – that guides our decisions.

It would be difficult to set up a satisfactory research project into the way teachers use theory in their lesson planning, though no doubt it would be possible. But the value of the results might be debatable, since it seems likely that different teachers working under different circumstances will make different uses of theory, and therefore generalisations drawn from the results might be of little real use. What seems to me likely to be more beneficial is that teachers should be aware of how they each individually make use of theory, so that they can assess whether they could profit by making changes.

Planning for teaching is a process of problem solving. The teacher sets goals (or has goals set by someone else), and looks for ways of achieving those goals. Of course, setting the goals is in itself a problem, and a problem which is solved with the help of theory. Furthermore, goals may be revised after attempting to solve the problem of how to achieve them, so we are talking about a rather complex process.

I describe below three models representing different ways in which teachers' existing body of theory might relate to the planning process. These models are offered merely as an aid to discussion of this relationship; they are derived only from observation of my own planning when working both alone and with other teachers, and have no research basis.

One way in which we might expect theory to function in planning is for it to act as a *processor*. Problems are specified, theory applied to them, and a solution turned out (Figure 2). There are types of theory that seem intended to work like this. For example, a rigid, prescriptive methodology (whether a published 'method' or a personal belief) might shape teaching in this way by specifying the stages to be included in the teaching of any language item or pattern. A teacher who uses a grammar/translation approach might thus automatically tackle any L_2 text by translating it into L_1. Another example would be the use of Munby's Needs Processor model (Munby 1978) in determining items to be taught in an ESP course.

It is clear that not all theory can be used in the 'theory as processor' model, since it only accommodates prescriptive theory, and it is far from being the case that all language teaching theory is prescriptive. Much language teaching theory is expressed in terms which are too qualified for it to be prescriptive, this reflecting recognition both of our incomplete knowledge of the learning process and of the fact that different learners in different learning situations react in different ways. Exclusive application of the theory as processor model would imply certainty that the theory was correct, and correct for all of a defined set of circumstances.

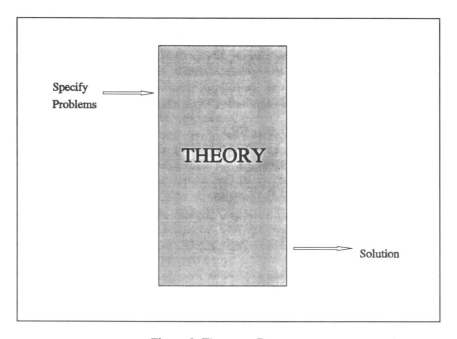

Figure 2. Theory as Processor

Not only will the theory as processor model only accommodate prescriptive theory, it will only accommodate certain types of prescriptive theory: namely, theories which are so formulated as to allow only one solution, or a very narrow range of solutions, to a given problem. Theories which, for example, only address certain aspects of a problem cannot so easily be fitted into the model, since they will not alone determine solutions. One can easily imagine language teaching theory of this type: prescriptive in implication, but yet not comprising a mechanism for producing solutions to problems. Such theory is more likely to be used prescriptively as an *arbiter*. For example, a theory that 'Entertaining classroom activities will promote learning more than unentertaining activities will' is prescriptive in that it clearly implies that classroom activities should entertain students. However, such a theory will not of itself produce a solution to a teaching problem. It will enable us to categorise ideas as 'acceptable' or 'unacceptable', in many cases giving a degree of acceptability, (e.g. 'fairly entertaining') or unacceptability ('extremely dull').

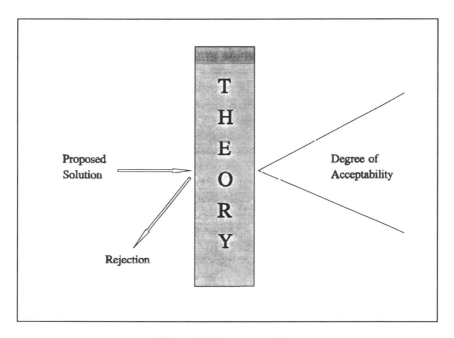

Figure 3. Theory as arbiter

In practice, application of theory as arbiter is likely to be much more complex than this, since a proposed solution to a teaching problem will probably be tested against not one but many theories – all those perceived as relevant.

The 'theory as arbiter' model may indeed represent part of the process that often goes on – consciously or unconsciously – in the process of planning language teaching. But since it cannot account for the generation of lesson content, it can only illustrate something close to the whole of the planning process when the source of teaching ideas is external to the teacher – for example, when all teaching ideas are drawn from published course material, and the teacher simply decides whether to use each suggestion or not.

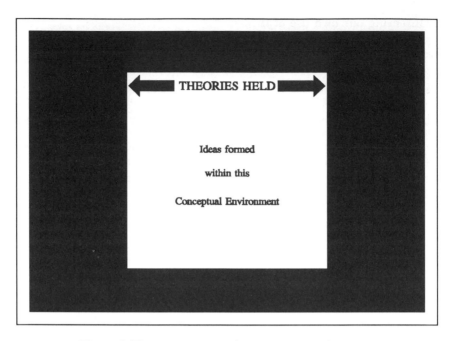

Figure 4. Theory as creator of a conceptual environment

A third way in which theory might be expected to operate is as *creator of a conceptual environment*. Each teacher, I have suggested, holds a set of theoretical assumptions or beliefs, built up from training, from reading, from experience, from thinking, perhaps from the teacher's own empirical research; some of these beliefs will be developed from others specifically for the particular case under consideration ('case theory'). These beliefs, I suggest, often define the conceptual boundaries within which the teacher normally develops ideas for classroom practice. We need such frameworks to enable us to think efficiently and effectively, since they prevent us from conceiving and considering ridiculous ideas for teaching. Furthermore, we could not expect to work efficiently on teaching planning if we built up this theoretical framework from scratch each time we worked on a new teaching problem (even if it were possible to discard all our previous ideas); we need to have an established conceptual environment within which we can work with confidence, and one which will enable us to develop and assess ideas quickly. Yet our conceptual frameworks are also likely to be restrictive, since they will tend to confine the range of options we produce for consideration.

4. Observing our own use of theory

It should be fairly obvious to us when we are using theory as a processor; as stated above, this will most often be in circumstances where we are adhering fairly strictly to a 'method' for some or all aspects of our teaching (e.g. audio-lingual method, Silent Way, Suggestopædia, etc.). Some teachers work in schools where this is required of them; others may decide themselves to adopt a particular methodology. At the outset of their teaching careers most teachers probably adopt a theory that 'the best way for me to teach my class will be to follow the instructions in the course book to the letter'; though crude, this 'theory' obviously produces a result in terms of a lesson plan!

Other patterns of use of theory may be rather harder to observe. Perhaps the circumstances in which we can most easily be aware of our own thought processes in lesson planning is when that planning is a joint activity – in team teaching, for example, or when working with a teacher who has a parallel class. In such circumstance teachers not only have to put forward ideas, they have to justify them as well. In such discussion one might expect the theory underlying our thoughts to be made explicit, and the process of planning to be more readily observable.

I have personally experienced three such teaching situations within the last few years. One was artificially engineered; it was organised as part of an M.A. course on which I was studying, and course participants were required to work in groups with classes for two lessons specifically in order for them to observe the way in which theory was (or was not) applied to practice. A second experience has been in working with two other teachers on preparing and teaching short courses of English for Danish lawyers; team-teaching and teaching in parallel groups have both been involved. Finally, I work closely with colleagues in planning teaching of parallel classes in language proficiency courses at university.

In all these instances, one of the first things to be done has been the establishment of some kind of working *case theory* – discussion of what the students are likely to want and need, what goals can probably be achieved in the time available, students' likely level of knowledge, motivation and language learning aptitude, etc. In other words, we discuss the distinguishing features of the group and the language and skills to be taught. Case theory is further developed as the course progresses and more is learned about the teaching; experiences are pooled and discussed, and decisions made about what will be considered desirable in the future.

I am quite frequently aware of theory being used as an arbiter in such joint planning sessions, and it is often this commonly-agreed case theory that is cited. Proposals for teaching ideas will be rejected because they teach language that falls outside the category of what has been defined as a useful teaching aim, or because they upset the balance of activities that we have agreed to be desirable, or because they do not fit in with the expressed wishes of the students. However, I am able to think of very few instances where 'authorities' have been specifically cited to support or reject a proposal, or indeed in establishing the case theory in the first place.

The fact that we have not had to build up all the theory on which our teaching is to be based in any of these three groups can only be explained by the existence of a considerable amount of common ground between the teachers before discussions of the particular cases in question started. Just as I have suggested that teachers each operate within an individual conceptual environment, so there are shared 'public' conceptual environments on which teachers working together depend. Within any given group of EFL teachers there will be an area of common ground, a set of assumptions and beliefs that are accepted by all in the group as axiomatic. When teachers work together, ideas which fit within their shared framework will be regarded as valid (i.e. worthy of consideration). Suggestions outside the shared field of beliefs will have to be justified, and if the public conceptual environment cannot be shifted to accept them, they will not even be considered as potential solutions to a teaching problem.

As an example, consider a hypothetical group of EFL teachers in Sweden working together to design a language course in the late 1960's. They would assume that they needed to identify structural items in the language for teaching. For any given structural item, they would automatically ask questions such as 'What will our *presentation* be like? What sorts of *drills* shall we use, and in what sequence? How can they be linked to some *freer practice*? What *writing exercises* shall we use as *consolidation?*' There would be no need for a member of the team to present an argument saying why there should be drills in this teaching sequence; it would be an element of the shared, public, accepted conceptual framework that drills were essential. Anyone suggesting, however, that perhaps drilling could be omitted would have to argue very cogently to even have his suggestion considered. By looking back at a public conceptual environment of the past, we can see its limitations; it is of course far harder to be aware of the limitations of our own present conceptual environments.

The action of theory as creator of a conceptual environment is not generally an observable process, and must to a large extent be assumed or inferred. While the occasions on which individual conceptual frameworks differ will be obvious, there is usually a high degree of overlap which goes virtually unnoticed. Without such shared views, joint planning would be virtually impossible. The effects of the existence such public conceptual environments are presumably far-reaching, yet I can call to mind only one example of an occasion when a design group became aware of those effects. After the lessons prepared as part of the M.A. course project, the regular class teacher commented that he was surprised that we had not asked students to write anything in the 'deep-end' activity[2] we used at the opening of the class, since the course was intended to be a pre-sessional academic writing skills course. In fact, students were not required to write anything at all during the first lesson; the first actual written production came in the homework between the two lessons. None of the team had felt that there was anything odd in this, or even noticed it, despite the fact that we were preparing materials for an academic writing course. It was as though we had all taken as axiomatic, without consciously considering it, that writing came late in the learning process.

It is when discussing ideas that fall outside the public conceptual environment that one realises how much one depends on it. One also comes to be aware of one's individual conceptual environment; when something one has always done automatically is suddenly challenged, one becomes aware that perhaps there are other ways of doing things. And when ideas are put forward that one has never thought of before, one becomes aware of a limitation. On one occasion, I had grave misgivings about the inclusion of an activity which required students working in pairs to perceive a pattern in a group of sentences, to formulate a provisional language 'rule' to account for it (without necessarily having to clearly express their rule for the teacher), and then to test their provisional explanation by applying it to an exercise. I was unable to conceive that such a task was within the capabilities of the students. While I was quite accustomed to an inductive approach, perhaps I felt that actually stating a language rule explicitly was the task of the teacher, not the student. Nevertheless, the use of the activity was strongly urged by one of the teaching team; it *was* used, and it worked very effectively, with students coming up with a variety of 'rule formulations' which enabled them to work through the language exercise correctly. As a result, my individual conceptual framework was extended.

In all the discussions I have participated in, it has been noticeable how rarely there is any citation of recognised 'authorities', of any statements of the type 'So-and-so suggests that x should be done in this type of situation'. It does happen; I have known specific reference to articles on marking of written work, reference to conference presentations, even reference to Krashen's Input Hypothesis as a way of justifying asking students to read more texts. Perhaps one reason for the rarity of these references is that one generally then has to expound and defend the original theory; for the reasons discussed in the introductory section, there are no authorities that are accepted without question. Instead, when any suggestion was challenged in discussion, the tendency was always first to cite experience as the justification for an idea; 'I've tried this, and it works' is a difficult argument to refute.

When I am planning alone, I am certain that I am similarly dependent on an established theoretical conceptual environment, and indeed I assume that this is true for all teachers. I also rely for the most part on classroom experience for my ideas, though on occasion I will draw on other sources – such as published methodological theory – to develop new teaching ideas.

In these ways, then, I believe that all the models of application of theory that I have described can represent a part of the planning process.

Conclusions

It would seem that application of theory as processor is only likely to be used in certain circumstances, in particular when a specific teaching method has been selected. This is no place to start a debate on the virtues of different 'methods', and such a debate would in any event be irrelevant to cases where teachers have no choice over the teaching methodology they are to use. However, I would argue that no method yet devised can convincingly be put forward as being appropriate in all situations (see Pennycook (1989) for a discussion of the concept of method and for further references; Pennycook argues that 'there is very good reason to be skeptical about methods' (p. 589)). We have no complete universal theory of language learning, and certainly no universal theory of language teaching. Indeed, much research has suggested that learners are different, and that they require different types of teaching. Methods, then, must be selected because they appear to be appropriate to particular students in a particular learning situation. Where teachers do themselves select a method for a teaching situation – perhaps just by choosing a particular course book, for example – I would suggest that the wider the teacher's knowledge, and the greater their ability to assess ideas critically, the better the chance that an appropriate choice will be made. Furthermore, the greater their knowledge of the theory behind the method selected, the more likely they are to be able to adapt it successfully to their individual students.

It seems that theory can be used as an arbiter, though its explicit use in this respect may be largely limited to case theory; I imagine that we rarely fully form (and need to test against an arbiter) a teaching idea which conflicts with our general teaching principles. The formulation of case theory is, I believe, an essential part of the teaching process; if we do not consider what we need to and are able to do with each group of students in each teaching situation, but simply treat every teaching case in roughly the same way, then we are probably moving too much towards a rather restrictive 'theory as processor' approach in which students regarded as the uniform objects to be processed by an unchanging teaching mechanism.

I have suggested that theory is important in its role as creator of a conceptual environment, both with respect to the private conceptual frameworks of individuals and the public frameworks accepted by those who share them. The individual body of theory which for each of us shapes our teaching planning conceptual environment and thus limits our normal idea-producing process is a compound of concepts and principles which we probably take for granted most of the time. We do not constantly recall it, mull it over, check it against original sources, challenge its validity. We may often not be aware that we *have* a view on a particular point; we have, perhaps, always done things in one particular way, and lack any awareness that there is an alternative.

We could not manage without these established conceptual environments. And if we spent too much time questioning the correctness of our basic theoretical principles the we would probably find we had neither the time nor the confidence to do much actual teaching. Furthermore, we might argue, if our students learn some language anyway, what would be the point of worrying too much about our own theories, as long as our practice 'works'? If we are drawing on current 'mainstream' ideas in the public conceptual environment current in our teaching situation, does it matter that we do not fully understand all the theoretical underpinnings of these ideas? In short, provided we do not find ourselves constantly lacking ideas which we are able to use in teaching, do we need to worry much about our basic theoretical assumptions?

I can find no simple answer to these questions. I believe that there are many EFL teachers doing a satisfactory job of teaching without fully understanding all the theory behind their methodology or materials. In a profession where there are many different teaching ideas on offer, and where new ideas are constantly being produced, too much knowledge of conflicting theories can be confusing, especially to the teacher at the beginning of his/her career. Teachers who have a tendency to jump uncritically on the latest methodological bandwagon may be abandoning adequate approaches for others that ultimately turn out to be less than satisfactory. However, I would also suggest that there are a great many teachers who are not doing as good a job of language teaching as they could be, and that part of the reason for this might be that their understanding of the thinking behind what they are doing is less complete than it could be.

I also feel – and again, I am drawing very much on my own experience – that our conceptual environments are never stationary. If we give up trying to expand our theoretical knowledge, then instead parts of it grow rusty with disuse; our conceptual area in which teaching ideas are produced grows smaller, leaving us with fewer resources with which to tackle different teaching challenges. I believe that we should always welcome the opportunity to examine new ideas, even if it is important that our examination should be a critical one, and that observed effectiveness in the classroom should be the touchstone by which we judge new thinking. We should not aim simply to expand our theoretical basis, but also to examine our existing assumptions regularly; this will involve making our theoretical frameworks 'explicit', in Ellis's term (1983:2). Are our own ideas about teaching at least coherent and rational, with some sort of underlying consistency? When a new teaching idea comes our way – perhaps one of the 'practical hints' mentioned by McDonough and McDonough – can we integrate it into our overall view, or is it filed away as a loose end, mentally labelled as 'another way of filling 30 minutes and keeping the class amused'?

In better understanding the thought behind the methods we adopt, in refining the theoretical criteria we use for judging teaching ideas, and most of all in maintaining and developing a theoretical conceptual environment that will help us to plan teaching effectively, I would stress the necessity for our own continuing teacher education and development – through reading, through seminars and courses, through involvement in research projects. Practical teaching experience is very important, but experience without the opportunity to examine the ideas of others surely cannot be enough. Nor should it ever be seen as the responsibility of teachers alone to find the time and resources to do these things in what is still in many instances a grotesquely underpaid profession; if teaching institutions want good results, they must be prepared to help their teachers by organising courses, by providing paid time off from teaching for attendance at in-service courses, by paying expenses for attendance at conferences, by providing libraries of books on teaching theory, and by facilitating research and stimulating a spirit of enquiry.

I have mentioned the need to expand conceptual environments, both individual and public; development comes through thinking what was once unthinkable. This, surely, is the job of the theorist: to develop new ideas. But we have already noted that the teacher – the practitioner – is also, by definition, a theorist, since theory is the thought underlying practice. Language teaching theorists need not necessarily be practitioners, but most are, or have been. Theory feeds practice, practice feeds theory; practice is applied theory, theory is, partially at least, analysed practice; the distinction between the two concepts never quite vanishes, but their intertwining makes them inseparable. In the terms in which we have discussed the relationship between theory and practice, it is far from the truth to suggest that theory is 'irrelevant' to practice; indeed, there could be no practice without theory. Any model of the relationship between theory and practice must take this closeness into account. Perhaps it is not too fanciful to suggest that the double helix might be an appropriate form for a model: theory and practice spiralling together towards ever greater things.

Notes

1. It should always be remembered, of course, that teachers are the practitioners only as far as teaching is concerned. What is really important in the classroom is learning, not the teaching that facilitates it; the practitioners of language learning are the students, not the teacher. Only within the last few years has any noticeable attempt been made to inform

the practice of learning by giving language students information about learning theory, and then only in a few cases and to a very limited extent (see, for example, Ellis and Sinclair (1989)). While there is much to discuss on the way in which and the degree to which theory informs practice in language teaching, the question of how much it currently informs language learning (as opposed to the question of how much it *should* inform language learning) would be quickly dealt with.

2. A 'deep end' activity is one in which students are asked to perform a language task without any preparatory teaching. By observing how successfully they can accomplish the task, the teacher can judge what language points need to be taught. Such activities can also make students more aware of their own language learning needs, and thus (one hopes) increase motivation and awareness in the learning process. learn.

References

Allen, J.P.B. and Corder, S.P. 1973. *Readings for Applied Linguistics* (The Edinburgh Course in Applied Linguistics, Vol 1). London: Oxford University Press.

Brown, H.D. 1980. *Principles of Second Language Learning and Teaching*. Englewood Cliffs, N.J.: Prentice Hall.

Chomsky, A.N. 1966. 'Linguistic theory', in *Language Teaching: Broader Contexts*. Report of N.E. Conference on Teaching of Foreign Languages. Menasha, Wisconsin. Extract reprinted as 'The utility of linguistic theory to the language teacher', in Allen and Corder (1973), pp. 212-224.

Ellis, Gail and Sinclair, Barbara. 1989. *Learning to Learn English: A Course in Learner Training*. Cambridge: Cambridge University Press.

Ellis, Rod. 1983. *Understanding Second Language Acquisition*. Oxford: Oxford University Press.

Freeman, Donald. 1989. 'Teacher training, development, and decision making: A model of teaching and related strategies for language teacher eduction'. *TESOL Quarterly* 23/1.

Ingram, D.E. 1980. 'Applied linguisics: A search for insight', in Kaplan (1980), pp. 37-56.

Kaplan, R.B. (ed.). 1980. *On the Scope of Applied Linguistics*. Rowley, Mass.: Newbury House.

McDonough, Jo and McDonough, Steven. 1990. 'What's the use of research?', *ELT Journal* 44/2, pp. 102-109.

McLaughlin, Barry. 1987. *Theories of Second Language Learning*. London: Edward Arnold.

Munby, J. 1978. *Communicative Syllabus Design*. Cambridge: Cambridge University Press.

Nunan, David. 1991. 'The teacher as decision-maker', talk given at the 25th IATEFL Conference in Exeter.

Pennycook, Alastair. 1989. 'The concept of method, interested knowledge, and the politics of language teaching', *TESOL Quarterly* 23/4, pp. 589-618.

Spolsky, B. 1978. *Educational Linguisitics: An Introduction*. Rowley, Mass: Newbury House.

Spolsky, B. 1980. 'The scope of applied linguistics', in Kaplan (1980), pp. 67-73.

Stern, H.H. 1983. *Fundamental Concepts of Language Teaching*. Oxford: Oxford University Press.

The Contributors

Hans Arndt is a lecturer in the Department of Linguistics at the University of Aarhus, Denmark. His main research and teaching interests are in the fields of pedagogical grammar, first and second language text production, syntax and pragmatics, and computer linguistics (the analysis of text corpora).

Tim Caudery teaches English Language Proficiency and Theory at the University of Aarhus, Denmark, having previously taught English to adults in Sweden and to teenagers in Cyprus. He has also long been associated with the Royal Society of Arts diplomas in language teaching, both as a teacher trainer and as an assessor. He is particularly interested in teaching and examining writing skills and in teacher training.

Glenn Fulcher is Director of English Studies at the English Institute, Nicosia, Cyprus. He is also at present a part-time research student with the University of Lancaster, working on oral language testing. Other research interests include language concordancing. He has published articles on a wide variety of topics within the field of TEFL.

Shen Shu Hung is Associate professor of English in the English Department, Bejin Foreign Studies University, where she teaches English Language and works on textbook development. Her major research activity is on the factors involved in language learning.

Stephen Keeler, formerly Director of Education at International House, London, is now a freelance language and education consultant. He has taught in Britain, Scandinavia, Eastern Europe and the Far East. He is the author of *Listening in Action* (Longman, 1988) and is currently working on several materials projects.

Shirley Larsen is a lecturer at the University of Aarhus, Denmark, where she teaches English Language Proficiency and Theory. Her recent research has been on translation, and she was the editor of number 19 in the *Dolphin* series, *Translation: A Means to an End* (1990). She is also particularly interested in the development of second langage writing skills.

Chris Moran is a freelance teacher trainer and writer. He has taught EFL in secondary, further and tertiary education both in the UK and in France, Spain, Germany and Yugoslavia. He is particularly interested in second language reading and has published a survey article in *Language Teaching* (with Eddie Williams) on the teaching of reading. Forthcoming articles will appear in *System* and *ELT Journal*.

Judith Munat is an English Language lecturer (*lettore*) at the University of Pisa, where her teaching and research are concentrated in the fields of reading, stylistics and discourse analysis. She previously held a similar post at the University of Palermo, and has also taught EFL at various universities in the United Kingdom.

Don Porter is Assistant Director of the Centre for Applied Language Studies, Universtiy of Reading, where he teaches Language Testing and Pedagogic Phonology, and is a member of the Language Testing and Evaluation Unit. He is co-editor (with Jack Upshur) of the international journal *Langauge Testing*, and has published widely on matters relating to language testing. He has taught English Language and Applied Linguistices in Pakistan, Syria, Egypt, Poland and Lancaster.

Althea Ryan lectures at the Department of Language and Communication at the Universtiy of Odense, Denmark. Her main research and teaching intrests are in the field of foreign language pedagogy. In particular, she is interested in the development of materials and methods for teaching writing, and in the way in which individual differences can be taken into account in the design of teaching materials and methods.

Brenda Sandilands is an editor of EFL teaching materials as well as being an EFL teacher. Now based in Oxford, she has previously taught ESL and EFL in Canada and Italy as well as Great Britain. She is particularly interested in the development of reading and writing skills.

Anna Trosborg is Reader in Communication Studies in the Department of English at Aarhus School of Business. Her current research interests are in the areas of pragmatics and Langauge for Specific Purposes, and her recent publications include various articles on negotiation strategies. She is co-author (with Jean McVeigh) of *Rules and Roles: A Workbook in Communication*.

David Vale is the author of the new activity-based *early bird* series for teaching English as a Foreign Language to children, published by Cambridge University Press. He has taught in more than 14 countries, and is currently developing various short training programmes for teachers of English to children.

Robert Wilkinson is currently employed by WorldNeth International Language Centre (post: Course Development and Training). His principal activities include ESP work at the University of Limburg (Faculties of Economics and Health Sciences) and with local firms. His main interests within ELT are learning motivation, evaluation, and English language change in Europe, hence his close involvement with the ELT network in Europe, *Networking English Language Learning in Europe* (NELLE). He has published several papers on these themes.

Abstracts

Airports or Whorehouses? Some Problems with Lexical Inferencing (Chris Moran)

Lexical inferencing is widely recommended as a reading strategy in both first and second languages. Traditional interest in the strategy has been intensified by research into cognitive skills and learning styles and strategies, and by models which have seen reading as a 'psycholinguistic guessing game'. Studies of vocabulary acquisition and reading in L_1 suggest that readers can infer the meaning of some unknown words, but it is not clear how far such evidence is applicable to reading in a second language. The few empirical studies on lexical inferencing in second language reading fail to provide convincing evidence that the meaning of a significant number of words can be inferred by learners. The author conludes that teachers and materials writers should be more cautious in recommending this strategy to second language learners.

Oral Assessment of L_2 Reading Comprehension (Judith Munat)

Assessment of receptive language skills – reading and listening – presents especial problems, since neither of these skills creates a directly observable result or product. The comprehension achieved can only be evaluated indirectly by making the test subject externalise his comprehension in some observable behavioural 'product'. Traditional methods of doing this, such as the production of written answers in response to comprehension questions or the answering of multiple-choice questions, may distort assessment, since skills other than reading comprehension are involved in the production of the assessed product.

This article reports on an experiment in the use of oral interviews conducted in L_1 on a text read in L_2 as a means of assessing reading comprehension. The test format is described in some detail, and band scales used in the test are presented. It is argued that the test offers a viable and valid alternative to traditional test types; in comparison with a standard multiple-choice reading comprehension test, it is argued that the oral interview has greater content and face validity. The practical advantages and disadvantages of the interview-based testing procedure are discussed.

Approaches to Teaching Writing (Brenda Sandilands)

The enormous amount of research on developing first and foreign language writing skills and the consequent plethora of approaches and materials has provided a complex and frequently contradictory body of literature on the subject. A close study of the major issues provides course designers with a variety of choices, enabling them to select those ideas which seem most appropriate for specific situations. This article surveys the literature on teaching writing in a foreign language, focussing on developments in the field during the past two decades and devoting particular attention to product-based and process-based approaches to teaching writing skills. It is argued that, in view of the greatly differing needs of individual writers, no one approach to teaching writing is comprehensive enough to be used to the exclusion of all others. An extensive bibliography is included.

Writing activities and Text Production in TEFL (Althea Ryan and Hans Arndt)

Full writing competence implies the ability to produce a range of types of written text for a range of different situations. This corresponds to the 'communicative competence' which is increasingly advocated for foreign language teaching in general, but is most often implemented in the teaching of spoken language. Full communicative writing competence ('text competence') thus involves more than simply 'code competence' (adequate control of syntax, morphology, spelling, punctuation etc.). The main purpose of this article is to demonstrate a didactic approach that may train several – in particular communicative – components of text competence, without resorting to excessive theoretical explanation.

The approach described permits focus on aspects of the match between formulation and situation, and at the same time on the revision phase, where this match is checked and refined more concentratedly than in any other phase of writing. In order to reach this phase it is normally necessary to go through pre-writing and writing first, but this article suggests a short-cut, namely the use of already existing texts. By choosing source texts of different types, analyzing them to determine how their situation is reflected in their formulation, and then manipulating aspects of either situation or formulation, it is suggested that it may be possible to build up step by step the competence required for text production.

Testing and Teaching Foreign Language Writing Skills at University Level
(Shirley Larsen)

The article describes the development of courses in teaching writing skills at the University of Aarhus Department of English, and the resulting changes in the examinations to which the courses lead. Students are now trained to take careful account of purpose, audience and medium in their writing. The main exercise type which has been used on the courses involves text transformation, where information and ideas are taken from an input text and used to create a new text intended for a different purpose from the original. The article describes various types of text transformation tasks which have been used, and assesses the benefits of the changes in the teaching that have been made.

The Role of Stylistics in EFL (Judith Munat)

This article addresses the problem of providing an English for Specific Purposes syllabus for foreign students of English Literature. Since literature can call upon any variety of English at one time or another, it would appear impossible to isolate a specialized 'language of literature'. Instead, it is suggested that the study of literature requires of students the ability to recognise as wide a variety of language types as possible, thus enabling them to make the link between authorial choice and the effect on the reader. An ESP course for students of English literature should encourage sensitivity to the range of styles, registers and text types offered by literary texts, stimulate curiosity about the way language is manipulated, and develop the capacity to understand the relationship between language choice and the factors determining such choices.

The article describes the syllabus for a Varieties of English course which has been developed over a period of five years at the University of Pisa. The detailed content and aims of three units of the syllabus are described. The syllabus is a flexible one which could be adapted to many teaching situations.

Using Mini-sagas in Language Teaching (Stephen Keeler)

The most interesting and successful teaching materials are those which are truly educational: materials which generate genuine, personal responses from students by speaking to and inter-relating with them at a personal level, and which involve them in activity which has some intrinsic value beyond the walls of the classroom. This article argues that mini-sagas provide a rich source of text and a genre for writing that can provide EFL teaching material of a type that will indeed fulfil these criteria.

A mini-saga is a story told in precisely fifty words – no more, no less. Originally presented in a writing competition run by the *Telegraph Sunday Magazine*, the mini-saga is a writing form which entertains and stimulates without being daunting or impossible to emulate. The article discusses the advantages of using mini-sagas in language teaching.

Request Strategies in Non-Native and Native Speakers of English (Anna Trosborg)

With the increasing demand for communicative competence in a second language, the interest in second/foreign language learning and teaching centres more and more on aspects of sociopragmatic competence and discourse competence. However, traditional classroom discourse does not generally promote these skills sufficiently in learners. Numerous studies have shown that a rigid pattern of classroom interaction and the frequent use of display questions leave learners little opportunity to develop these important aspects of communicative competence.

This paper describes a study comparing the use of request strategies by native and non-native speakers of English. Danish learners of English displayed shortcomings in both sociolinguistic competence and discourse competence. It is argued that this finding supports the case for the teaching of sociopragmatic skills in the second language classroom.

Sex, Status and Style in the Interview (Don Porter and Shen Shu Hung)

The paper describes a study which sought to provide evidence that two variables significantly affect the assessment of spoken language by interview, namely the sex and the status of the interviewer. It was hypothesised that assessment scores would be higher when the interviewer was female, and when the interviewer was presented to the interviewee in such a way as to suggest relatively lower status. Data was collected from 56 interviews, half with male and half with female interviewers, half with 'boosted status' and half with 'non-boosted status' interviewers. No evidence was found to suggest that status affected interview performance, though this may have been because the experimental design did not create a sufficiently marked difference in perceived status of the interviewers. However, evidence was found to support the hypothesis that the sex of the interviewer significantly affected assessment scores. It was further found that interviewers whose language displayed features often regarded as characteristic of 'female speech style' produced significantly higher scores from the interviewees, irrespective of the actual sex of the interviewer.

Teaching English to Children – An Activity-Based Approach (David Vale)

It is not sufficient to provide children, whether native or non-native speakers, with a programme of study which merely focuses on language, or indeed on any other isolated skill. Instead, it is necessary to offer a whole learning situation in which language development is an integral part of the learning taking place, and not only the end product.

The article describes an activity-based approach to teaching children which, it is suggested, integrates language learning into a whole learning experience. Teaching principles and techniques are discussed, and examples of lesson content provided.

The Role of Assessment by Teachers in School (Glenn Fulcher)

This article reports on two studies conducted between 1988 and 1990 into the reliability and validity of teacher assessment of students in school. It begins by predicting that with changes in educational assessment in the United Kingdom it is likely that course work or some other form of assessment internal to the overseas institutions will be introduced as an option in EFL and ESL examinations. The University of Cambridge Local Examinations Syndicate has already built this into its International General Certificate of Secondary Education ESL examination. However, it must be asked whether or not teachers' assessments (a) provide valuable information on student abilities which cannot be provided by more formal modes of assessment or testing, and (b) are reliable.

Using a range of formal examinations and internal assessment procedures as part of a developmental programme at the English Institute, Nicosia, Cyprus, the validity and reliability of teacher assessment within this one institution was studied in the hope that it may prove useful (in terms of results and experimental design) for researchers in other parts of the world concerned with the development of internal assessment procedures.

The article concludes with recommendations for other institutions wishing to operate internal assessment procedures which may contribute to the final 'end-product' assessment of student abilities in a second or foreign language, and for the examination boards which are actively engaged in developing and marketing such schemes of assessment.

Innovation and Development in English in Europe (Robert Wilkinson)

The thrust of the argument in this paper is that the growth of English in Europe is subject to the same factors that drive growth in industry, innovation and selection. The paper treats Europe as a multimarket situation in which the dominant language, English, is in the most favourable position to innovate and expand. The selection factor is related to the relative efficiency of language expressions, with least-efficient expressions being selected out over time. Alongside these factors are community and individual level factors, the former of which denote activities in other language groups and actions by international organizations, the latter denoting factors such as communication needs, cultural differences and identity. The paper contends that these factors will have a considerable influence on the evolution of a pragmatic variety of English in Europe and indicates a number of areas of potential change, as well as the concomitant implications for EFL teaching.

Theory and Practice in Language Teaching (Tim Caudery)

The relationship between theory and practice in TEFL remains a subject which engenders much discussion. Many teachers appear to have a hostile or ambivalent attitude towards 'theory'. The article presents a series of models which are intended to facilitate the discussion of the ways teachers use 'theory' in planning their teaching. It is argued that teachers of EFL should be prepared to actively examine the theoretical assumptions underlying their own teaching practice.